Lifelines 4

COPING SKILLS IN ENGLISH

SECOND EDITION

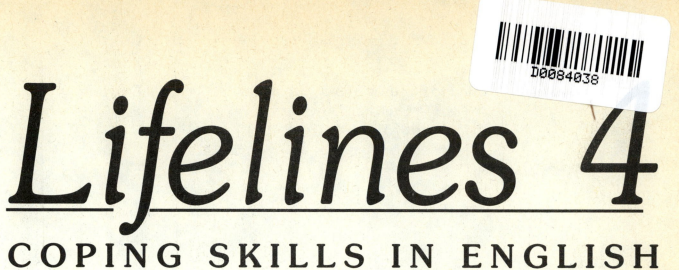

Barbara Foley
Howard Pomann

Institute for Intensive English
Union County College, New Jersey

PRENTICE HALL REGENTS, Englewood Cliffs, New Jersey 07632

This series is dedicated to our dear friend and colleague, Gretchen Dowling
Gretchen Dowling
8/31/43–4/13/89

Acquisitions editor: Nancy Leonhardt
Production supervision: Noël Vreeland Carter
Interior design: A Good Thing and Jerry Vota
Cover design: Jerry Vota
Illustrations: Don Martinetti, D.M. Graphics, Inc.
Manufacturing Buyer and Scheduler: Ray Keating

Photo Credits:
Laima Druskis, Units 1, 10, 12, and 14; Abraham Feria, Units 2, 6, 11, and 13; U. S. D. A., Unit 3; Interbank, Unit 4; Irene Springer, Unit 5; Hakim Raquib, Unit 7; Ken Karp, Unit 8; American Cancer Society, Unit 9.

Source material, Unit 3, courtesy of U.S.D.A., Human Nutrition Information Service

© 1995 by PRENTICE HALL REGENTS
Prentice-Hall, Inc.
A Paramount Communications Company
Englewood Cliffs, New Jersey 07632

Printed in the United States of America
10 9 8 7 6 5 4 3 2 1

ISBN 0-13-097544-3

Prentice-Hall International (UK) Limited, *London*
Prentice-Hall of Australia Pty. Limited, *Sydney*
Prentice-Hall of Canada Inc. *Toronto*
Prentice Hall Hispanoamericana, S.A., *Mexico*
Prentice-Hall of India Private Limited, *New Delhi*
Prentice-Hall of Japan, Inc. *Tokyo*
Simon & Schuster Asia Pte. Ltd., *Singapore*
Editora Prentice-Hall do Brasil, Ltda., *Rio de Janeiro*

Contents

Introduction

Barbara Foley and Howard Pomann have devised this survival skills series specifically for entry-level adult students who need to learn basic skills and basic language in order to function effectively in the United States. The Conversations and practices lead students through carefully controlled exercises to the point where they can "put it together" for themselves. In addition to whole-class and large-group activities, LIFELINES features many small-group activities which allow the teacher to step aside and became a facilitator as the students work together using the language in new and different ways. The focus on coping skills and functional language, rather than grammar and vocabulary, promotes learning by increasing student interest. The repetition of the same basic exercise formats throughout, allows students to concentrate on learning language, not exercise formats. Gretchen Dowling's excellent "To the Teacher" section gives clear explanations of how to do each exercise, along with an abundance of ideas for adapting them to your own individuals needs. Photographs, drawings and realia bring the content of each unit to life for students. LIFELINES really makes learning easier for your students, and teaching easier for you.

Sharon Seymour
Alemany Community
College Center
San Francisco

To the Teacher

LIFELINES is a four-book ESL coping skills series for adult learners at entry, beginning, low-intermediate, and intermediate levels. Each book deals with ten or more different coping skill areas. The series is competency-based and integrates the coping skills with the essential language forms, vocabulary, and cultural information needed in each situation.

Skill areas are reintroduced throughout the series with different competencies. For example, in "Telephone," in Book 1, students ask to speak with someone; in Book 2, they leave a simple message; in Book 3, they give and take a longer message; in Book 4, they ask for information and leave a message on an answering machine. Those competencies requiring simpler language forms come before those calling for more difficult ones. Thus, grammatical points such as verb tenses are introduced in appropriate sequence. They are reintroduced cyclically throughout the series and via the different contexts within each book.

The series is suitable for a wide variety of adult and secondary school classes. It could be the total program, for example, for open-entry ESL classes of 3-6 hours per week. For intensive language courses, it would be one strand of the total program. In community college or secondary school classes, it could be used either to reinforce grammatical structures, or to introduce them in context.

Each unit is self-contained, takes approximately two hours, and affords practice in listening, speaking, reading, and writing. The table of contents for each book lists the coping skill areas, the functions or competencies, and the main grammatical structures in each chapter. This gives the teacher easy access to the information needed to choose how best to integrate LIFELINES with individual programs, classes, and teaching styles.

This series incorporates both whole-class and small-group learning activities. All the activities are designed to give students as much "inner space" as possible to process the language according to their own individual learning styles. Those for the whole class are to introduce or sum up the structure, vocabulary, and cultural information needed to perform the coping skill; those for the small groups, to provide students with the intensive independent practice they need to make the language their own.

In the whole-class activities, the teacher utilizes stories, pictures, and conversations to introduce the new language and information in the chapter. Although the teacher is leading the activity, the activities are designed so that the teacher can easily elicit the correct language with minimal teacher modeling.

In smaller group activities, the teacher's role is that of a small-group facilitator assisting the students in completing their tasks, rather than of a leader. Depending on the activity and level of the students, a teacher can circulate from group to group, stay with one group, or sit separately from the groups and assist only when asked.

Students working in small groups learn to discover their own mistakes, to correct each other, to share opinions, to experiment with the language, and to work as a learning community. Small groups allow the teacher to divide the class according to particular language needs, and to work with students having individual problems as well as those who are ahead of the class. They also free students to ask questions they may not ask in the whole-class setting.

For the teacher, one of the biggest advantages of LIFELINES is that small-group work, and accommodation to different learning styles, are built-in. It is not necessary to supplement the books with small group tasks in order to meet individual student needs. The small-group activities have been tested with a wide variety of students. They work without extra work for the teacher.

Naturally, there are many ways to handle the activities presented in the workbooks, depending on students' proficiency levels, and the teacher's personal style. In the pages which follow, the authors offer "how to" suggestions which have proven effective for them. These are intended simply as some ways to structure classwork so that students have maximum opportunity to meet their own learning needs in a productive and secure atmosphere. They are not intended as limits on the readers' style or creativity.

WHOLE CLASS ACTIVITIES

Discuss

Discuss
The Discuss questions and accompanying illustration or photo set the scene for the unit. The class should talk about the illustration and what they see happening in the picture. The Discuss questions help the student to relate their personal opinions and experiences to the theme of the unit. Cultural comments and explanations can be made at this time. During this introduction to the unit, the focus is on expanding the students' knowledge of the coping skill rather than the correction of grammar.

Read
A short factual reading introduces the main cultural theme of each of each unit. Students read the story silently twice. In the first reading, students should concentrate on the general ideas of the passage and not try to understand every word or to analyze the structures. During the second reading, students should concentrate on understanding and interpreting the materials. After the students finish reading, they complete the true/false exercise which focuses on the main ideas and supporting details. Once this exercise is completed, the class discusses the new vocabulary, clarifies the main concepts, and expands on the content.

Listen, Read and Say

Listen, Read and Say
This is the dialogue which introduces the language and competency. It is the core from which all the other activities and expansions of the chapter emerge.

First, the student should read the dialogue to themselves. They should ask about the meaning of any new vocabulary or expressions. Then, the teacher models the conversation with natural speed and intonation, with the students repeating each sentence as a whole class. Finally, students should be given a few minutes to practice the dialogue with a partner. The teacher can ask one or two partners to present the dialogue to the class.

Practice

This activity introduces new vocabulary within the previously established context and grammatical structures. A single sentence or interaction from the dialogue is given as the model. Students practice the model, substituting the vocabulary cued by the pictures below it. Students should practice all the substitutions with a partner. The teacher should circulate, answering any questions and helping with pronunciation as necessary.

Step 1: If much of the vocabulary is new, students can repeat each item in isolation, chorally and then individually, following the teacher's model.

Step 2: The teacher elicits the use of the new items within the model sentence or interaction. One way to do this is simply to have the students repeat the complete utterances after the teacher. This is a good first step, especially for very low-level classes. After this initial security is given, however, students need a little more independence.

A variation, or follow-up, is for the teacher to give only the first utterance as a model. The teacher then simply points to or calls out the number of each different picture and has the students give the complete utterance. This can be done both chorally and individually.

Step 3: Students can then continue practicing all the substitutions, with the person sitting next to them. The teacher can circulate, helping with pronunciation as necessary.

Step 4: To further reinforce the pronunciation of the new vocabulary, follow the procedures described in Step 4b of Listen, Read, and Say.

SMALL-GROUP ACTIVITIES

Before beginning the small-group activities, the teacher divides the students in groups of two to five depending on the activity and the size of the class. The teacher then goes over the directions carefully and demonstrates what each student will do, explaining what the teacher's role will be, whether circulating from group to group, or staying with one group. The teacher should give the students a time frame; for example, telling the students they have fifteen minutes to complete the task. The time frame can always be extended. Clear information about what to expect helps students feel secure and be more productive.

There are many different ways to group students. Some teachers like to have students of the same ability together; others to mix them so the more advanced can help the slower. Some like to mix language backgrounds in order to encourage the use of English; other have the same backgrounds together in order to raise the security level, or to facilitate students' explaining things to each other. Some like student self-selection so that working friendships may develop more easily; others don't see this as crucial to the development of supportive, productive groups. Each teacher's values and pedagogical purposes will determine the way the class is divided into groups.

Partner Exercise

This small-group activity is designed for two students to practice a specific grammatical structure in a controlled interaction. The left-hand column of the Partner Exercise gives word or picture cues from which Student 1 forms a statement or question. The right-hand column gives the complete sentences. Student 2 looks at this column, using it to be "teacher" and check the utterances of the other student.

Students are to fold the page in the middle so that S1 is looking at the left-hand column and S2 at the right.

Step 1: Students form into pairs of students.

Step 2: Students fold their pages and do the exercise.

Step 3: The teacher can circulate from group to group assisting when asked or needed, encouraging students to listen carefully and to correct each other's sentences and pronunciation.

Step 4: When a pair has completed the exercise, the two students should change roles and do it again.

Complete

Completion activities provide writing practice and the use of individual cognitive skills. Students are asked, for example, to complete sentences, write questions, fill in forms, find and apply information from charts or maps, etc. Directions are specific for each activity. To explain and structure the activities, the teacher can use the chalkboard. As the students write individually or in small groups, the teacher circulates, giving assistance as needed or requested.

Interaction

The Interaction Charts give the students a structured opportunity to practice their new language with one or two other students. Each activity begins with two or more questions about the topic.

Step 1: Students sit with a partner and ask each question. They mark their partner's response on the chart, usually by recording a "yes" or "no," circling an appropriate response or writing a few words. The students then switch roles. Often, other language and questions emerge as the students interact. The teacher should encourage the students to speak freely and gain confidence in their language use.

Step 2: Repeat Step 1 with a different partner. Most interaction charts ask the students to speck with two students.

Step 3: After the students have their partners' responses, several students should report their information back to the class. Typically, the teacher will ask a student, "Who(m) did you speak to?" and "What did he tell you?" The goal in this activity is correctly reporting information and using the new vocabulary. Do not focus on the correctness of the grammar.

Putting It Together

The last two pages in each unit give the students the opportunity to practice and expand the coping and language skills emphasized in the units' more open-ended conversation. In most chapters, a problem-solving situation is introduced with a short reading and a detailed illustration. As a whole class or in small groups, students read the problem aloud, discuss the picture, and answer a series of questions to become familiar with the situation and the issues surrounding it. Students then have the opportunity to discuss their opinions and suggest solutions to resolve the problem through various small group discussion and writing activities.

Role Play

A Role Play or Go Find Out is the final activity. With a role play, the students work together as partners and write a conversation about the coping skill area. The students have the support of the previous activities to help create the dialogue. The teacher circulates, giving assistance as needed and requested. The students practice the conversations without looking at their papers, and then stand in front of the class and act out their conversations. Whenever this kind of freedom is given, a teacher may expect less perfection in students language than during controlled practice.

Go Find Out

In the Go Find Out students are asked to find out specific information about services, agencies or businesses in their communities. For the next class, students report their findings to the other students.

Gretchen Dowling
Barbara H. Foley
Howard Pomann
John McDermott

Acknowledgments

The development of this series has been the result of a long growth process. We wish to thank our many friends and colleagues who have given their support, shared their ideas, and increased our insights into the language-learning process and its application in the ESL classroom:

John Chapman, Ralph Colognori, Joyce Ann Custer, Mary Dolan, John Duffy, Jacqueline Flamm, Irene Frankel, Susan Lanzano, Joann LaPerla, Darlene Larson, Nancy Liggera, Fred Malkemes, Joy Noren, Douglas Pillsbury, Deborah Pires, Sherri Preiss, Jennybelle Rardin, Sharon Seymour, Earl Stevick, George Yates and the faculty at the Institute for Intensive English, Union College. Particular thanks to John McDermott for the revision and editing of the chapter readings.

A special thanks goes to our parents, Muriel and Warren Haedrich and Evelyn and Julius Pomann for their encouragement and love.

Barbara Foley
Howard Pomann

1 How Have You Been?

Discuss

How much time do you spend
studying each week?
What are some reasons why you don't
have enough time to study?
What are some obstacles to finding
enough time to study?
How can you find more time to
study?

Read

Like most students, you may find
that time is one thing you never seem
to have enough of. Using good time
management can help you be more
successful in school and work. First, analyze your commitments. How many
hours do you need for study, work, family commitments, recreation, and rest? How
can you find more time and decide the best times to study without shortchanging
other important parts of your life?

Scheduling is one key. Try to identify your "peak" energy hours when you
have the most energy and think most clearly. Arrange your schedule so you can
study then, and use times of the day when you are tired for recreation and
relaxation. Also, look for times when you can squeeze in small study tasks. Write
out a schedule and follow it carefully.

It is also necessary to control interruptions including visitors, family members,
telephone calls, and noise. You should try to have a quiet place to study. Turn off
the TV and radio while studying. Politely but firmly let people know that your
studies are important, and learn to say "No" when someone asks you to do
something for them.

Additionally, procrastination is a real obstacle to managing time. There are
ways to fight it. To complete larger assignments, divide the work you need to do
into smaller chunks and feel the accomplishment as you finish each one. Tell
yourself how great you'll feel when you've finally finished the whole project.

Read each sentence. If it is true, write T. If it is false, write F.

_____ 1. Make a list of things to do each day and schedule all your important
tasks for the week on a calendar.

_____ 2. It is best to study when you have finished all your jobs and can relax.

_____ 3. It is only useful to study when you have a large block of time.

_____ 4. When you have a report due, you should plan to do it in parts.

_____ 5. Although you have a class to attend tomorrow, you should agree to
pick up your sister at the airport.

Ana: Gloria! Hi. How are you?

Gloria: Busy. In fact, too busy. I've been studying English, working full-time, taking care of the kids . . . Not a minute for myself.

Ana: How's school going?

Gloria: I've been struggling because I just can't find the time to study. Everybody is always asking me to do something.

Ana: You're just going to have to say "No" sometimes.

Practice this model with the pictures below.

> A: How have you been?
>
> B: Busy. I've been _____ *studying English* _____ .

1. study English

2. paint the apartment

3. prepare for my exams

4. go out with someone new

5. put in a new bathroom

6. work part-time

Practice this model with the activities below.

A: How's _____ **Maria** _____?

B: Good./Not so good./Busy.

_____ **She** _____ 's been _____ **looking for a job** _____.

A: How're _**your parents**_ ?

B: Good./Not so good./Busy.

They've been _____ **taking care** _____

_____ **of my daughter** _____.

1. Maria
   look for a job

2. your parents
   take care of my daughter

3. your brother
   work two jobs

4. your aunt and uncle
   get ready to move

5. Carlos
   worry about his family

6. your parents
   go to night classes

7. your brother and sister
   study English

8. David
   have trouble with his kids

9. Luis and Olga
   go through a divorce

10. Carmen
    visit friends in Texas

11. Joseph and Ana
    look for a smaller apartment

12. Gloria
    feel tired and run down

Partner Exercise

Describe each person's activities.

<table>
<tr><td>Student 1
I / work part time
I've been working part time.</td><td>Student 2
Listen carefully and help Student 1.</td></tr>
</table>

Student 1	Student 2
1. I / work part time	1. I've been working part time.
2. My daughter / study hard	2. My daughter's been studying hard.
3. My sister / look for a new job	3. My sister's been looking for a new job.
4. My parents / get ready to move	4. My parents have been getting ready to move.
5. I / see someone new	5. I've been seeing someone new.
6. My son / take guitar lessons	6. My son's been taking guitar lessons.
7. My mother / be on a strict diet	7. My mother's been on a strict diet.
8. They / visit friends in Florida	8. They've been visiting friends in Florida.
9. I / paint the house	9. I've been painting the house.
10. We / walk three miles a day	10. We've been walking three miles a day.

(FOLD HERE)

Complete these conversations.

1. Ron: I haven't seen you for a while. How have you been?

    Dave: _____. I've been _____.

    Ron: How about you? You look great!

    Dave: Thanks. I've been _____.

2. George: Hi, Carmen.

   Carmen: Hi, George. How are the kids?

   George: Good, thanks. Katie _____,

            and Emily _____.

3. Linn: Kim, how are you? I haven't seen you for months!

    Kim: I've been really busy. _____

            _____.

            And how about you?

    Linn: _____

            _____.

5

Make a schedule for your next week's activities. Indicate blocks of time for school, work, study, household chores, sleep and recreation. Talk about your schedule with a partner. What changes could you make to use your time more effectively?

	Sunday	Monday	Tuesday	Wednesday	Thursday	Friday	Saturday
6 A.M.							
8 A.M.							
10 A.M.							
12 P.M.							
2 P.M.							
4 P.M.							
6 P.M.							
8 P.M.							
10 P.M.							
12 A.M.							
2 A.M.							
4 A.M.							

Interaction

Ask another student these questions about the time chart on the facing page. Fill in the chart below with information about your partner's schedule and your schedule.

	You	Your Partner
What hours do you go to school?		
What hours do you work?		
What hours do you sleep?		
What hours do you study?		
What is the best time of day for you to study?		
Where do you study?		
What interruptions do you have?		
When do you have free time?		
What do you do in your free time?		

Putting It Together

Sit in a small group. The following sentences give several suggestions about the effective use of study time. After you read each one and discuss it, write "should" or "shouldn't" in the blank. You may all have different answers, so explain your reasons to the group.

1. You _____ write a detailed schedule of your week's activities.

2. You _____ study at the school library rather than at home if possible.

3. You _____ go home immediately after class to study.

4. You _____ study during breaks at work or breaks in other activities.

5. You _____ adjust your schedule if your plans change.

6. You _____ work full time and go to school full time.

7. You _____ miss a week of classes because one of your relatives is sick and everyone else in your family is too busy to help.

8. You _____ miss a day of classes to help a relative get a driver's license.

9. You can't get started with a report that is due soon. You _____ take a break and come back later to try again.

10. While you are studying, your mother asks you to go shopping with her. You _____ go.

2 Used Cars

Discuss

Did you ever buy a used car? Who did you buy it from?
How did you check out the car before you bought it?
Does your state require auto insurance?

Read

When you need a car, you may decide you want to buy a used car. A used car is much cheaper and can be a good investment. However, you must be careful not to buy a "lemon," a car with a lot of problems. You need to decide what price car you can afford and what size car you need. Then, shop around carefully, using newspapers, car dealers, or people you know. Find out "how much car" your money can buy.

To help you determine the best used car for the best price, you also should go to the library and look in consumer magazines. These magazines will show the retail and wholesale "book value" of cars, listing a range of acceptable prices depending on the condition of the car. These magazines will also list the repair records of most cars for the past few years. If the type of car you are thinking of buying has a poor repair record, be careful.

Before you buy a used car, you should inspect it carefully, test drive it, and take the car to a good mechanic for a thorough inspection. Then you are ready to negotiate the price. Be sure to get a written receipt for any money that you give the seller. Remember, the seller must transfer the title of ownership to you. Then, you must register the car with the proper state agency. Most states require automobile insurance.

Read each sentence. If it is true, write T. If it is false, write F.

_____ 1. You can check your local newspaper to find a used car.

_____ 2. The price of a used car is negotiable.

_____ 3. Most used cars have the same repair records.

_____ 4. The repair records and prices listed for used cars in consumer magazines are accurate.

_____ 5. If you buy a used car from a neighbor, take the car to a mechanic before you purchase it.

Carla: I'm back again. Last month the car stalled every time I stopped. And this week it overheats when I'm in heavy traffic.

Mechanic: I'm not surprised. I told you last time, it really needs a new engine. And the fuel pump needs to be replaced soon.

Carla: I can't believe how much money I'm spending on repairs.

Mechanic: Well, the car is 12 years old and has over 120,000 miles. I don't think it's worth repairing anymore.

Carla: I think you're right. I think I'd better start looking for something else.

Practice this model with the car repairs below.

It needs (a) new _____*radiator*_____.

The _____*radiator*_____ *is* shot/gone.

It looks like you need (a) new _____*radiator*_____.

1. radiator

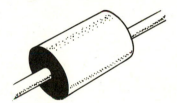

2. muffler

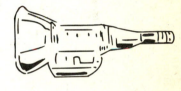

3. transmission

4. brakes

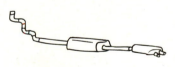

5. exhaust system

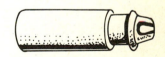

6. starter

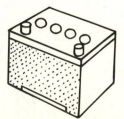

7. battery

8. fuel pump

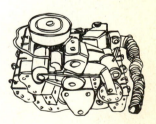

9. engine

Practice this model. Use a phrase from Column A and a phrase from Column B to describe different car problems.

It _____***stalls***_____ when _____***I accelerate***_____.

Column A		Column B
It _____	when	_____.

Column A

doesn't start
stalls
hesitates
overheats
lacks power
backfires
pulls to the right
makes a strange noise

Column B

I stop
I step on the accelerator
I drive over 50 mph
it's hot / cold / raining
I accelerate
I turn
I go up a hill
I'm in heavy traffic
I'm in stop and go traffic
I step on the brakes

Use a phrase from Column A and a phrase from Column B above. Write five car problems.

1. _____

2. _____

3. _____

4. _____

5. _____

Interaction

Answer the questions below about your own car. Then find out about a partner's car. Fill in the information on the chart below.

	Your car	Your partner's car
What kind of car do you have?		
What year is it?		
Who fixes your car?		
What problems do you have with your car now?		
What problems have you had with your car since you bought it?		

Saul: Can you tell me about this station wagon?
Owner: Sure.
Saul: What year is it?
Owner: It's a '93.
Saul: How many miles does it have?
Owner: About 67,000.
Saul: How many miles does it get per gallon?
Owner: About 18.
Saul: How does it run?
Owner: It's in great shape. It has a new transmission and new front tires.
Saul: How much are you asking?
Owner: $7,300.
Saul: I'd like to take it to a mechanic.
Owner: Sure. Let me know when.

Practice this model with the vehicles below.

A: What year is your _____ *van* ?	B: It's a _____ '94 .
A: How many miles does it have?	B: About _____ 58,000 .
A: How many miles does it get per gallon?	B: About _____ 14 .
A: How much are you asking?	B: _____ $7,200 .
A: How does it run?	B: _____ *Great*! .

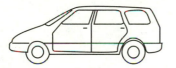

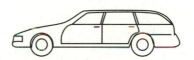

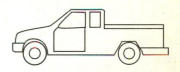

1. van '94
   58,000 / 14
   $7,200

2. station wagon '92
   72,000 / 15
   $6,300

3. pickup '95
   30,000 / 17
   $14,000

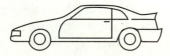

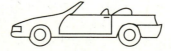

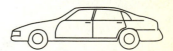

4. sports car '93
   52,000 / 22
   $10,700

5. convertible '91
   84,000 / 21
   $5,200

6. car '94
   42,000 / 26
   $12,700

These abbreviations are often found in classified ads for cars in the newspaper. Match each abbreviation with the correct word on the right.

mi	condition
pb	miles
ps	air-conditioning
ac	power brakes
pw	door
cond	good
exc	power windows
dr	power steering
gd	roof
rf	1,000
bo	cylinders
K	speed
spd	excellent
cyl	best offer

Role play

CADILLAC '91 DeVille 71,000 mi. One owner. Garaged. pb/ps/ac Excellent cond. $6,800 272-1954	FORD 1993 Mustang GT. Black, 5 spd, fully loaded, P/S, P/B, P/W, alarm system. Mint cond. 26K mi. Asking $9,200. Call Dave 789-2148	MERCURY Sable SL 1994 - 6 cyl, garaged, loaded, 32 K mi. Like new $14,500. 376-0381
CHEVY CAMARO RS 1992 60K mi, new exhaust, exc cond, $7,900 354-8162	FORD Bronco II 1992, V6, a/c, auto, 47K mi, ps,pb,am/fm, $6,500 call 232-7309	OLDSMOBILE '92 Cutlass Ciera - V6 A/C, new tires & muffler, 85K mi, gd cond, $4,200. 815-9221
DODGE '93 Caravan Grand SE, low miles, exc cond, all options, $10,200/bo. Call 249-0136	HONDA CIVIC ' 94 2dr 4spd ac am/fm/cass 43K mi, Original owner $8,300 Call after 5pm 459-9254	TOYOTA CAMRY V6 XLE 1995 18K mi, loaded, all pwr sun rf, air bag, CD stereo, alarm $18,200. 654-8097

Read the classified ads above. Choose one or two cars that you would like to see and test drive. With another student, write and practice a conversation between a potential buyer and a car owner. Find out as much information as you can about the car and ask if you can take it to a mechanic to check it out. Present your dialogue to the class.

You want to sell your car. Write a classified ad to place in your local newspaper.

You are looking for a used car. You have looked at three mid-sized cars that are four years old. You like the features and the driving performance of all of them. You are looking in a consumer's magazine for each car's Frequency of Repair Record. You want a reliable car that will not cost much in repairs.

	Vega	Lyra	Antares
Price	$7,000	$10,000	$11,000
Mileage	58,000	64,000	50,000

FREQUENCY OF REPAIR RECORD

1 = poor   2 = fair   3 = average   4 = very good   5 = excellent

	Vega	Lyra	Antares
Engine	3	5	4
Fuel system	4	5	4
Ignition system	2	4	3
Transmission	3	5	3
Electrical system	3	5	4
Steering	3	5	4
Brakes	1	4	3
Exhaust system	4	5	5
Air conditioning	4	5	2
Body rust	2	5	3
OVERALL	**2**	**5**	**3**

Sit in a small group. Look at the Frequency of Repair Record above and discuss these questions.

1. Which car is the most expensive?
2. Which car is the least expensive?
3. Which car has the least mileage?
4. Which car has the best transmission?
5. Which car has the most engine problems?
6. Which car has the worst repair record?
7. What are the major problems with the Vega?
8. Which car would you buy? Explain your reasons.

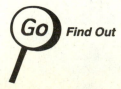

Find Out

Choose a used car from an ad in the newspaper. Then, go to your school or local library and use a consumer magazine or reference guide. Find out information about the specific make, model and year car you are interested in. What is the frequency of repair record? What is the car's safety record? What problems might the car have? What is the price range? Report your information to the class.

3 A Healthy Diet

Discuss

How many meals do you eat a day?

Do you usually prepare American food or food from your native country?

What changes do you need to make in your diet?

Read

Planning nutritious meals isn't easy. It takes time and involves making choices. Good eating habits can help you feel better, look better, and have more energy. The following guidelines can help you choose a diet that is both healthful and enjoyable.

• Eat a variety of foods. It is the best way to get the energy, protein, carbohydrates, vitamins, minerals, and fiber you need for good health.

• Maintain a healthy weight. Being overweight increases your chances of developing high blood pressure, heart disease, stroke, certain cancers, and the most common type of diabetes.

• Avoid too much fat, especially saturated fat. A diet low in fat helps reduce your weight and lessens your risk of heart attack and certain types of cancer. Fat has twice the number of calories of carbohydrates and proteins.

• Choose a diet with plenty of vegetables, fruits, and grain products. They are high in nutrients, but generally low in fat and calories. Also, they contain fiber which helps food move through the digestive system.

• Use sugar only in moderation. Sugar and highly sweetened food are high in calories and are limited in vitamins and minerals. Sugar also contributes to tooth decay.

• Use salt and sodium in moderation. For many people, blood pressure rises with higher sodium intake.

• If you drink alcoholic beverages, do so in moderation. Alcoholic beverages are high in calories, but supply few vitamins or minerals. Drinking is linked with many health problems.

Read each sentence. If it is true, write T. If it is false, write F.

_____ 1. The chance of having a heart attack is increased if you are overweight.

_____ 2. Saturated fats increase your risk of heart attack.

_____ 3. Low-fat foods have less calories.

_____ 4. Grain products, such as bread and rice, are high in fat and calories.

_____ 5. Alcoholic beverages have few calories.

Before you begin this unit on nutrition, think about your own diet and answer these questions.

How often do you eat	Seldom or never	1 or 2 times a week	3 or 4 times a week	Almost daily
1. Two or more kinds of fruit or fruit juice a day?				
2. Citrus fruits and juices (e.g. oranges or grapefruit)?				
3. Three or more different kinds of vegetables a day?				
4. A dark-green leafy vegetable, such as spinach or broccoli?				
5. Starchy vegetables like potatoes, corn or peas?				
6. At least six servings or breads, cereals, pasta or rice a day?				
7. Two servings of lean meat, poultry, fish or alternatives such as eggs, dry beans or nuts per day?				
8. Cooked dry beans or peas?				
9. Foods made from whole grains, such as whole-wheat bread or oatmeal?				
10. Two servings of milk, yogurt or cheese per day?				

If you checked *Almost Daily* or *Three to Five Times a Week* for most items, you are eating foods from the five food groups. Your diet is sufficiently varied and you are receiving the vitamins, minerals, and protein that your body needs.

How often do you eat or drink. . . .	Less than once a week	1 or 2 times a week	3 or 4 times a week	Almost daily
1. Fried, deep-fat fried or breaded foods?				
2. Fatty meats such as sausage, lunch meats, or steak with heavy fat?				
3. Whole milk, hard cheese, or ice cream?				
4. High-fat desserts, such as pies and cakes?				
5. Rich sauces or gravies or regular salad dressing?				
6. Butter or margarine on your vegetables or toast?				
7. Soda, fruit drinks or punches?				
8. Desserts sweetened with sugar, such as cookies or ice cream?				
9. Candy?				
10. Jam, jelly, or honey on bread or rolls?				

If you checked *Three to Five Times a Week* or *Almost Daily* for several items, your diet may be too high in fat and sugar. You do not need to eliminate these foods from your diet, but you may need to eat them less often and in smaller amounts.

15

The Food Pyramid is a guide to what you should eat each day. It lets you choose a healthy diet that's right for you. In the lower section, there are five major food groups. You should eat foods from each of these groups for a balanced diet with the vitamins and nutrients you need. No one group is more important than the others. You need them all for good health. On the top of the pyramid are fats, oils, and sweets. These are foods like butter, cream, cake, and cookies. You should only consume a small amount of these ingredients.

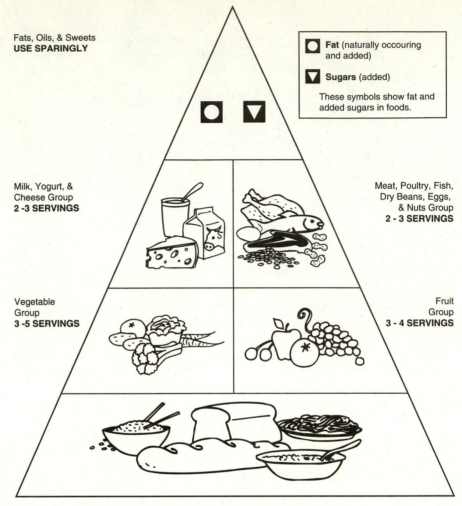

Fats, Oils, & Sweets
USE SPARINGLY

○ **Fat** (naturally occouring and added)

▽ **Sugars** (added)

These symbols show fat and added sugars in foods.

Milk, Yogurt, & Cheese Group
2 -3 SERVINGS

Meat, Poultry, Fish, Dry Beans, Eggs, & Nuts Group
2 - 3 SERVINGS

Vegetable Group
3 -5 SERVINGS

Fruit Group
3 - 4 SERVINGS

Bread, Cereal, Rice, & Pasta Group
6 -11 SERVINGS

Food Pyramid courtesy of USDA, Human Nutrition Information Service

 *Complete*

Complete this chart. List all the food you ate yesterday or the food you eat on a typical day. Remember to include foods such as oil, butter or mayonnaise.

BREAKFAST	LUNCH	DINNER	SNACKS

Read

The amount of food that counts as a serving is listed below. Some food belongs in two or more groups. For example, a large piece of pizza belongs in the bread group (crust), the vegetable group (tomato sauce) and the milk group (cheese).

Food Group Servings

Bread, Cereal, Rice and Pasta — 6 to 11 servings		
1 slice of bread	1 ounce of cereal	1/2 cup of cooked cereal, rice or pasta
Vegetable — 3 to 5 servings		
1 cup of raw leafy vegetables	1/2 cup of other vegetables, cooked or chopped raw	3/4 cup of vegetable juice
Fruit — 2 to 4 servings		
1 medium apple, banana, or orange	1/2 cup of chopped, cooked or canned fruit	3/4 cup of fruit juice
Milk, Yogurt, and Cheese — 2 to 3 servings		
1 cup of milk or yogurt	1-1/2 ounces of natural cheese	2 ounces of process cheese
Meat, Poultry, Fish, Beans, Eggs, and Nuts — 2 to 3 servings		
2-3 ounces of cooked lean meat, poultry or fish	1/2 cup of cooked dry beans, 1 egg, or 2 tablespoons of peanut butter count as 1 ounce of lean meat	

complete

Look at your diet on the facing page. Complete the pyramid and write how many servings you had from each food group. Remember, a large portion is two or more servings. If you ate a cup of rice, that counts as two servings.

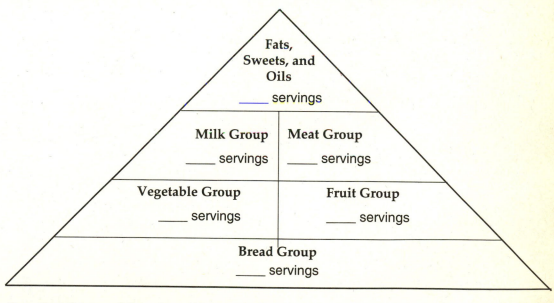

Practice
Practice

Practice this model and analyze your diet.

I ate _____ servings from the _____ group.

I should eat more _____.

I should eat less _____.

17

Practice this model. Match each situation with an exercise suggestion.

If you're out of shape	you could, you should why don't you	_walk_.

1. If you're out of shape,

2. If you're in great shape,

3. If you want to be alone,

4. If you like company,

5. If you hate to sweat,

6. If you love the indoors,

7. If you love the outdoors,

8. If you have joint problems,

9. If you don't have much time,

10. If you're easily bored,

11. If you're competitive,

12. If you can't spend much money,

How could you fit more exercise into your busy day? Write four more suggestions for your lifestyle.

1. **I could use the stairs instead of the elevator.**_____.

2. _____.

3. _____.

4. _____.

5. _____.

Discuss

Answer these questions about suggested weights for adults. The lower weights usually apply to women; the higher weights usually apply to men.

Suggested Weights for Adults		
Height[1]	Weight in pounds[2]	
	19 to 34 years	35 years or older
5'0"	97–128	108–138
5'1"	101–132	111–143
5'2"	104–137	115–148
5'3"	107–141	119–152
5'4"	111–146	122–157
5'5"	114–150	126–162
5'6"	118–155	130–167
5'7"	121–160	134–172
5'8"	125–164	138–178
5'9"	129–169	142–183
5'10"	132–174	146–188
5'11"	136–179	151–174
6"	140–184	155–199
6'1"	144–189	159–205
6'2"	148–195	164–210
6'3"	152–200	168–216

[1] Without shoes
[2] Without clothes

Permission to use information in chart courtesy of National Research Council, National Academy of Sciences

1. How much should a woman who is 5'5" tall and 35 years old weigh?

2. What should a man who is 5'6" tall and 40 years old weigh?

3. What should a woman who is 22 years old and 5'0" weigh?

4. How much should a man who is 6'3" tall and 30 years old weigh?

5. How tall are you? Find the suggested weight for your age. Do you need to gain or lose any weight?

Practice

Depending on your age and the amount of exercise you do, you need between 1,600 and 2,200 calories a day. Fat intake should range from 53 to 73 grams daily. Look at the two meals below. Use the model and compare the amount of fat and calories in each item and in the complete meal.

Higher Fat Meal

	Calories	Grams of Fat
Fried chicken leg	220	12
French fries, 10 strips	160	8
Green beans, 1/2 cup with butter, 1 teaspoon	30	4
Whole milk, 1 cup	150	8
Apple pie, 1 slice	400	19
Total =	**960**	**51**

Lower Fat Meal

	Calories	Grams of Fat
Baked chicken leg	170	8
Baked potato, 1 medium	100	0
Green beans, 1/2 cup plain	30	0
2% low fat milk, 1 cup	120	5
Baked apple, 1 large	80	0
Total =	**500**	**13**

_____ has   more   fat   than_____.

less   calories

19

Some foods are higher in calories and fat than other foods. When buying food and planning meals, your food choices can make a big difference in nutrition. Use the model to talk about the information in the chart below.

	Calories	Grams of Fat		Calories	Grams of Fat
Skim milk, 1 cup	86	trace	American cheese, 1 oz	105	9
1% Low fat milk, 1 cup	102	3	Cheddar cheese, 1 oz	115	9
Whole milk, 1 cup	150	8	Mozzarella cheese, part skim, 1 oz	80	5
Baked potato, plain	100	trace			
Baked potato with tbsp of butter	200	11	Low fat yogurt, 1/2 cup	105	2
French fries, 20 strips	320	8	Ice Cream, 1/2 cup	135	7
			Sherbet, 1/2 cup	135	4
2 tbsp creamy Italian dressing	140	16	Butter, 1 tbsp	100	11
2 tbsp regular Italian	140	14	Margarine, 1 tbsp	100	11
2 tbsp reduced calorie Italian dressing	30	4	Mayonnaise, 1 tbsp	100	12
			Olive Oil, 1 tbsp	120	14
			Vegetable Oil, 1 tbsp	120	14
Whole wheat bread, 1 slice	60	1	Apple, 1 medium	80	trace
Doughnut, 1	245	11	Apple pie, 1 slice	400	19
Banana	104	1	Broccoli, 5 oz	40	1
Peach	36	trace	Carrots, 1/2 cup	24	trace
Orange	65	trace	Corn, 1/2 cup	90	1
			Green beans, 1/2 cup	30	trace
Ground beef, 3 oz	250	18	Lettuce, 1/2 cup	4	trace
Steak, 3 oz	185	9	Potato, 1 medium	100	trace
Ham, 3 oz	175	11			
Chicken, dark meat, 3 oz	165	7	Flounder, 3 oz	60	1
Chicken, light meat, 3 oz	140	3	Shrimp, 3 oz	90	2

There are **250** calories in **3 ounces of ground beef** .

There are **18** grams of fat in **3 ounces of ground beef** .

There are more calories in **ground beef** than in **chicken** .

There is more fat in **ground beef** than in **chicken** .

Discuss

Mayonnaise

Nutrition Facts
Serving Size 1 tbsp (15 g)
Servings Per Container 64

Amount Per Serving	
Calories 100	Calories from Fat 100

	% Daily Value*
Total Fat 12g	18%
Saturated Fat 2g	10%
Polyunsaturated Fat 7g	
Cholesterol 5 mg	2%
Sodium 70 mg	3%
Total Carbohydrate 0g	0%
Dietary Fiber 0g	0%
Sugars 0g	
Protein 0g	

Not a significant source of Vitamin A, Vitamin C, Calcium, or Iron.

INGREDIENTS: Soybean oil, eggs, vinegar, water, egg yolks, salt, sugar.

* % Daily Value shows how a food fits into the overall daily diet.

Reduced-Calorie Mayonnaise

Nutrition Facts
Serving Size 1 tbsp (15 g)
Servings Per Container 64

Amount Per Serving	
Calories 50	Calories from Fat 45

	% Daily Value*
Total Fat 5g	8%
Saturated Fat 1g	5%
Polyunsaturated Fat 2g	
Cholesterol 5 mg	2%
Sodium 80 mg	3%
Total Carbohydrate 1g	0%
Dietary Fiber 0g	0%
Sugars 0g	
Protein 0g	

Not a significant source of Vitamin A, Vitamin C, Calcium, or Iron.

INGREDIENTS: Water, soybean oil, food starch modified, distelled vinegar, egg yolk, salt.

* % Daily Value shows how a food fits into the overall daily diet.

Answer these questions about each label.

1. What is a serving size?
2. What are the ingredients in this product?
3. Is this a product you sometimes buy?
4. What brand of this product do you usually buy?
5. How many calories are in a serving?
6. How many grams of fat are in a serving?
7. How many grams of saturated fat are in a serving?
8. Is a serving of this food high or low in fat?
9. How much cholesterol is in a serving?
10. Is a serving of this product high or low in cholesterol?
11. How much sodium is in a serving?
12. Is this product high or low in sodium?

Discuss

Food Preparation Tips to Reduce Total Fat, Saturated Fatty Acids, and Cholesterol

1

Steam, boil, bake, or microwave vegetables rather than fry. Or, for a change, stirfry in just a small amount of vegetable oil.

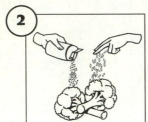

2

Season vegetables with herbs and spices instead of fatty sauces, butter, or margarine.

3

Try flavored vinegars or lemon juice on salads or use smaller servings of oil-based or lowfat salad dressings.

4

Use a vegetable oil in place of solid shortening, margarine, and butter whenever possible. Try using les oil than short-ening in baked products.

5

Try whole-grain flours to enhance flavors of baked goods made with less fat an cholesterol-containing ingredients.

6

Replace whole milk with lowfat or skim milk in puddings, soups, and baked products.

7

Substitute plain lowfat yogurt or blender-whipped lowfat cottage cheese for sour cream or mayonnaise.

8

Choose lean cuts of meat and trim fat from meat before/or after cooking. Remove skin from poultry before or after cooking.

9

Roast, bake, broil, or simmer meat, poultry, or fish rather than fry.

10

Cook meat or poultry on a rack so the fat will drain off. Use a non-stick pan for cooking so that added fat is not necessary.

11

Chill meat or poultry broth until the fat becomes solid. Spoon off the fat before using the broth.

12

Limit egg yolks to one per serving when making scrambled eggs. Use additional egg whites for larger servings.

13

To lower cholesterol, try substituting egg whites in recipes calling for whole eggs. Use two egg whites in place of each whole egg in muffins, cookies, and puddings.

Information courtesy of the USDA, Agricultural Research Service

1. Which of these suggestions do you already follow when you cook?
2. Which of these suggestions would be difficult to follow with your style of cooking? Why?
3. Which of these suggestions would be easy to follow with your style of cooking? Why?
4. Which of these suggestions will you try to use when you cook?

Putting It Together

Ingredients

1 tbsp olive oil
1 medium onion, cut into chunks
1/2 clove garlic, minced
1 red pepper, diced
3 cups of broccoli flowerettes
2 skinless, boneless chicken breasts,
        cut into 1" pieces
2 tbsp low sodium soy sauce
1/3 cup water or chicken broth
1 tsp cornstarch

Directions

Heat oil in skillet.
Stir-fry onion and garlic for 1 minute.
Add red pepper and broccoli and stir fry for 3 more minutes.
Add chicken and continue to stir fry for 8 to 10 minutes.
In a small bowl combine the soy sauce, water, and cornstarch. Pour this
mixture over the chicken and vegetables and stir until the sauce thickens,
1 or 2 more minutes.
Serve over rice.

*Share a favorite low-fat recipe with the class. Make it at home first and measure
the amount of each of the ingredients carefully.*

Recipe

Ingredients:

Directions:

4 Credit Cards

Discuss

Do you have a credit card? How did you apply for it?
When do you use it?
How do you feel about using a credit card?

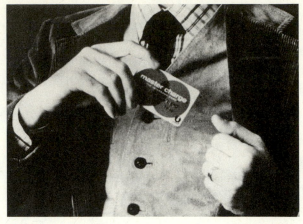

When you make a purchase in a store, you can usually pay for the item in cash or with a credit card. Credit cards have some advantages over cash. For one thing, you do not have to carry large amounts of cash with you when you go shopping. You also do not have to pay for the items that you charge until the monthly bill is due. If you pay the whole balance at the end of the month, you do not have to pay any interest. Another advantage is that if you have a problem with the merchandise, you can stop the payment by calling the card company.

One disadvantage to using a credit card is that people sometimes spend too much money because they do not have to pay in cash. Then, when they can not pay their total balance at the end of the month, they have to pay high interest rates on their balance. Some people have large credit card balances. They can only afford to pay the interest, so they can't get out of debt for a long period of time.

It is not difficult to get a credit card if you have a steady job and a good credit history. Pay your rent, phone, and utility bills on time. Open a checking or a savings account. If you don't have a credit history, talk to a bank officer about getting a small loan to establish credit. Once you decide to get a card, try to find a card that has no annual fee and low interest charges. Not all cards are the same. Research the best card for your situation.

Read each sentence. If it is true, write T. If it is false, write F.

_____ 1. If you pay your credit card balance at the end of each month, you still have to pay a finance charge.

_____ 2. Most stores will accept a credit card for payment.

_____ 3. If you have difficulty controlling your spending, it is better to pay in cash.

_____ 4. A person with a bad credit history will have difficulty getting a credit card.

_____ 5. A person who pays all his bills on time and has an account in a bank can usually get a credit card.

Listen, Read and Say

Todd: The bill is $65. Should we pay cash or charge it?
Ann: Let's use the credit card. I need the cash for tomorrow and I don't want to go to the bank.
Todd: How much should we leave for the tip?
Ann: Fifteen percent is about $10.
Todd: I'll add the tip to the bill.
Ann: That's fine.

Practice this model with the bills below.

This receipt is from _____**Fashions Plus**_____ .

The date of the bill is _____**12/21/95**_____ .

_____**Todd**_____ paid $ **98.00** for _____**clothing**_____ .

SALES DRAFT

FASHION PLUS
MOUNTAIN AVENUE
WARREN, NJ 07090

8496936398596746 36547
Terminal 333874855

12/21/95
US 5254 5678 2222 6666
Exp 3/99
Inv. 3444498
Auth. Code 20009
Amount $98.00

X
Todd Bowman

I agree to pay the total amount
of this bill on my credit card.

DATE: 12/21/95
TIME: 17:32

**ROCKY'S SERVICE
CENTER**
**411 Morris Avenue
Summit, NJ 07901**

Transaction #859 442 981
Auth. # 63381
Acct. #5254 5678 2222 6666
Exp. 3/99

DESC _____**gas**_____

TOTAL $_____**18.00**_____

Signature: *Todd Bowman*
THANK YOU

CARDHOLDER AGREEMENT

CARDHOLDER AGREES
TO PAY THE TOTAL
AMOUNT SHOWN
BELOW.

SIGNATURE: *Todd Bowman*

DATE: 12/23/95
TRANS. NO. 43381
TIME: 18:33
APPROVAL: 05219
CARD #5254 5678 2222
6666
EXP: 3/99

SALE $132.43
**DRAKE HOTEL
200 BROAD STREET
WESTFIELD, NJ
07090**

5254 5678 2222

CHARLIES DINER
253 ELMER ST
WESTFIELD NJ 07090

SIGN HERE

X _ *Todd Bowman*

Dinner				
DATE 12/21/95	AUTHORIZATION 045185		SUB TOTAL	45 90
			TAX	2 75
WORLD WIDE	5023625		TIP MISC	7 00
			TOTAL	55 65

CUSTOMER COPY

CUSTOMER: KEEP THIS COPY FOR YOUR RECORDS

*Practice these models with the information below from Todd's credit card statement. Ask questions with **What, When,** or **Where.** Then ask the price.*

| _____What_____ did he _____buy_____ ? He _____bought tickets_____ . |
| How much _____were they_____ ? _____They were $268_____ . |
| or |
| How much did _____they_____ cost? _____They_____ cost $_____268_____ . |

| 5/17   Midwest Airlines | $ 268.00 |

| 5/20   Little Italy Cafe | $ 51.74 |

| 5/17   Gateway Motel | $ 148.00 |

| 5/21   A Plus Electronics | $ 279.18 |

| 5/18   The Music Box | $ 37.95 |

| 5/23   Jay's Jewelry | $ 89.44 |

Complete these questions about Ann's credit card purchases.

Date of Trans	Date of Post	REFERENCE#	TRANSACTION	AMOUNT
6/7	6/7	56158787559	Central Airlines	299.00
6/10	6/11	56159946328	Safeco Car Rental	65.00
6/11	6/11	56161298475	Sam's Seafood Restaurant	45.60
6/12	6/14	56165386007	Dallas Motel	124.87

1. When _____*did she buy airline tickets*_____ ?   on 6/7.

2. How much _____ ? $299.00.

3. When _____ ?   on 6/10.

4. How much _____ ? $ 65.00.

5. Where _____ ?   at Sam's.

6. How much _____ ? $ 45.60.

7. Where _____ ?   at the Dallas Motel.

8. How much _____ ? $124.87.

Sit in a small group. Discuss the credit card statement below and answer the questions.

CREDIT CARD STATEMENT

ACCOUNT NUMBER	PAYMENT DUE DATE	PAST DUE AMOUNT	SCHEDULED PAYMENT	MINIMUM PAYMENT DUE	PLEASE INDICATE AMOUNT PAID	NEW BALANCE
5254 5678 2222 6666	10/15	157.20	25.00	25.00		710.85

Todd and Ann Bowman
1323 Front Street
Winston, Delaware 13872

Date of Trans	Date of Post	REFERENCE#	TRANSACTION	AMOUNT
9/12	9/12	62358675432	Northern Airlines	137.60
9/15	9/15	62359836274	Kenny's Shoes	37.00
9/15	9/16	62359879450	Chan's Restaurant	25.75
9/16	9/17	62360166743	Atlas Car Rental	64.52
9/17	9/17	62360168712	Tops T-Shirts	32.00
9/15	9/17	62361889335	Holiday Motel	135.86
9/17	9/18	62362911749	Charlie's Clothing	118.60

NO FINANCE CHARGE WILL BE CHARGED FOR PURCHASES IF THE NEW BALANCE IS PAID IN FULL WITHIN 25 DAYS OF THE BILLING DATE	CREDIT LIMIT	PAST DUE AMOUNT	BILLING DATE	DAYS IN BILLING CYCLE	PAYMENT DUE DATE	MINIMUM PAYMENT DUE
	2000	157.20	9/20	32	10/15	25.00

PREVIOUS BALANCE	PAYMENTS	CREDITS	PURCHASES AND CASH ADVANCES	LATE AND/OR OVER LIMIT CHARGES	FINANCE CHARGES	NEW BALANCE	ANNUAL PERCENTAGE RATE
357.20	200.00	0.00	551.33		2.32	710.85	17.79

1. How much do Todd and Ann owe on their credit card this month?

2. When is the bill due?

3. What is the minimum payment they can pay this month?

4. What will happen if they don't make a payment this month?

5. What are a few of their expenditures this month?

6. What is their credit limit?

7. How much was their previous balance from September?

8. What was the finance charge on the previous balance?

9. How much did they put on their credit card this month?

10. What is the annual percentage rate?

Sit in a small group. The following sentences give opinions about credit cards and money. After you read each one and discuss it, decide if you agree or disagree with the statement.

	Agree	Disagree
1. All adults should have a major credit card.	_____	_____
2. It's easy to obtain a credit card.	_____	_____
3. You need to establish credit before you can obtain a major credit card.	_____	_____
4. Interest rates on credit cards are low.	_____	_____
5. You should pay your total credit card balance every month.	_____	_____
6. If someone steals your credit card and uses it, you are responsible for paying for the purchases.	_____	_____
7. Most stores will accept a credit card for payment.	_____	_____
8. Most stores will accept a personal check for payment.	_____	_____
9. It's dangerous to carry more than $200 in cash.	_____	_____
10. It's better to pay with cash than with a credit card.	_____	_____
11. When you have a credit card, it's easy to spend too much money.	_____	_____
12. You should pay for your new TV with a credit card.	_____	_____

Putting It Together

Kumiko and Toshi have been saving for a living room set for a year. They have $2,200 in the bank, their total savings. In a reputable furniture store, they saw the perfect set, consisting of a sofa, a love seat, and two chairs. The sale price is $1,999. They need the furniture, but are worried that if they buy the furniture, they won't have enough money for an emergency or a big bill.

Discuss Kumiko and Toshi's situation. Should they buy the furniture? Choose one of these options below, then explain your reasons.

_____ Wait and buy the furniture in the future.

_____ Buy the furniture with their savings.

_____ Buy the furniture with their credit card and pay it off slowly.

_____ Buy the furniture with a lay-away plan.

_____ Buy the furniture with their credit card and pay it off at the end of the month.

_____ Pay $1,000 from their savings and put the rest on their credit card.

Reasons:_____

_____

_____

_____

Sit in a small group. Figure out these math problems about paying by credit card.

1. Sandra paid $585 for a new TV. She paid off the TV over six months. The total interest was $48. What was the real cost of the TV?

2. Tran charged $2,384 dollars in purchases last year. He made payments totaling $2,732 for principal and interest for the year. How much interest did he pay for the year?

3. The previous balance on Alex's credit card was $641. Last month he sent in a payment of $285. This month he charged $93 more in new purchases. What is his new balance?

4. The yearly interest on a credit card is 18%. What is the monthly interest rate?

5. The monthly interest on Maria's credit card is 1.5%. If her unpaid balance is $500, how much interest will she pay this month?

Interaction

Fill in the information about a credit card you have. Then, ask another student these questions about a credit card and complete the information below.

	You	Your Partner
1. Do you have a credit card?		
2. What do you charge with your card?		
3. Do you pay your card off at the end of every month?		
4. What's the interest rate on your card?		
5. Is there an annual fee for your card?		
6. Do you get any rebates from your card?		

Go **Find Out**

Pick up an application for a store credit card or a major credit card. What kind of financial information do you need to provide?

5 A Car Accident

Discuss

Have you ever been in a car accident? Describe the accident. Did the police come? What did they do?
Whose fault was the accident?

Read

Statistics tell us that sooner or later all of us, as drivers or passengers, will be involved in motor vehicle accidents. If you have an accident, there are several things that the law requires. First, you must always stop. Never leave the scene of an accident. If there is damage to the cars, or someone is hurt, you must report the accident to the police. It is important that all drivers wait for the police to give information for the police accident report. While you are waiting for the police to arrive, exchange driver's licenses, car registrations, and insurance card information. Also write down names and telephone numbers of witnesses.

You must report the accident to your insurance company as soon as possible, even if it wasn't your fault or if the damage seems minor. Be very careful about trying to settle with the other driver without reporting the accident. The other driver may promise to pay for the damage, but later decide not to.

If someone is hurt, do not move the person from the vehicle. Wait for the police or ambulance squad. In most states, hospital and doctor bills from an accident are paid by the insurance companies. If someone is hurt, the person should see a doctor and consult with a lawyer about possible legal action.

Read each statement. If it is true, write T. If it is false, write F.

_____ 1. You must give your insurance information to the other driver when you are involved in an accident.

_____ 2. Only report an accident to your insurance company if someone is hurt.

_____ 3. The police will only come if someone is injured.

_____ 4. You should always try to negotiate a settlement with the other driver.

_____ 5. If someone is hurt, the injured person has to pay his or her own medical bills.

Listen, Read and Say

Police:	What happened?
Mr. Lee:	I was driving through the intersection when that driver jumped the red light and hit me.
Ms. York:	That's not right. I had the green light. He went through the red light.
Police:	Was anybody hurt?
Mr. Lee:	No, just shaken up.
Police:	I need your license, registration, and insurance card.

Practice / Practice

Practice this model with the accidents below.

A: What happened?

B: I ____**was driving through the intersection**____ when ___**she**___ ____**passed the stop sign**____ and hit me.

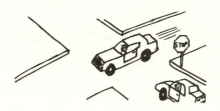   

1. drive through the intersection   pass the stop sign

2. make a left turn   go through the red light

3. drive in the middle lane   cut me off

4. go down the street   pull out of a parking space

5. drive along the highway

come into my lane

6. drive along the street

back out of that driveway

Use a phrase from column A and a phrase from column B. Describe three accidents.

A	B
go through an intersection	go through a stop sign
go down the street	jump the red light
stand at a red light	pull out of a parking space
turn right	back out of the driveway
make a left turn	cut me off
drive in the right lane	come into my lane
drive along	fall asleep

1. _____ *I was driving along when he pulled out of a*

parking space and hit me. _____

2. _____

_____

3. _____

_____

4. _____

_____

Practice **Practice**

Practice this model with the chart below. Describe the damage to this car.

A: What was the damage to your car?	
B: My _____*windshield*_____ was __*smashed*__ .	

bumper
fender
hood
light
grill
windshield
roof
door
side
trunk
car

dented
scratched
smashed
crushed
damaged
totaled

Interaction

Ask a partner about a car accident. Fill in the answers on the chart below.

Did you ever have a car accident?	
What happened?	
What were the road conditions?	
Whose fault was the accident?	
Was anyone hurt?	
What was the damage to the cars?	
Did your insurance cover the damage?	

ACCIDENT REPORT

DATE OF COLLISION	TIME	STREET	NEAREST INTERSECTING STREET
August 12	2:50 p.m.	Broad St.	River Road

VEHICLE 1		VEHICLE 2	
DRIVER'S NAME Tom Vickers		**DRIVER'S NAME** Alya Parcheck	
ADDRESS 35 Benson Place Tampa, Florida		**ADDRESS** 68 Flamingo Drive Tampa, Florida	
DRIVER'S LICENSE NUMBER 4639 00914 278 365		**DRIVER'S LICENSE NUMBER** 7894 2951 2821 604	
OWNER'S NAME Tom Vickers		**OWNER'S NAME** Carl Parcheck	
ADDRESS same		**ADDRESS** same	
MAKE AND MODEL 1995 Toyota Camry		**MAKE AND MODEL** 1993 Ford Taurus	
VIN NUMBER 90042079862154		**VIN NUMBER** 68733012911348	
INSURANCE COMPANY All Safe		**INSURANCE COMPANY** State Pro	
POLICY NUMBER 665 AH 3278		**POLICY NUMBER** ST 518 367	

PERSONAL INJURY ☐ Yes ☑ No   AMBULANCE ☐ Yes ☑ No   TICKET ISSUED ☑ Yes ☐ No

NAME: _____   NAME: _____   NAME: _Alya Parcheck_

DIAGRAM

River Rd.

Broad St.

\#1

\#2

Stop Sign

N / W / E / S (compass)

WEATHER _clear_

DESCRIPTION OF ACCIDENT

Driver # 1 states that while heading east on Broad Street, at the intersection of River Road, Vehicle # 2 failed to stop at stop sign and struck Vehicle # 1. Driver # 2 states that while heading north on River Road, she failed to stop at the stop sign, entered intersection, and struck vehicle # 1.

OFFICER'S SIGNATURE _Richard Gomez_

Discuss these questions.

1. When was the accident?
2. What time was the accident?
3. What were the weather conditions?
4. Where was the accident?
5. Who were the drivers?
6. How did the accident happen?
7. Which vehicle did not stop?
8. Did the drivers agree about how the accident happened?
9. Was anyone hurt?
10. Did either driver receive a ticket?

Sit in a small group. Decide which procedures you should follow if you have an accident. After you read each sentence and discuss it, write "should" or "shouldn't" in the blank.

1. You _____ leave the scene of an accident if there is no damage to your car.

2. You _____ exchange your license, registration and insurance card with the other driver.

3. You _____ argue with the other driver about whose fault the accident was.

4. You _____ wait for the police to come and fill out an accident report.

5. If you have a small accident, you _____ wait for the police.

6. You _____ get out of the car if you are hurt.

7. You _____ let the ambulance take you to the hospital if you are hurt.

8. You _____ call your insurance company as soon as possible.

9. You _____ report the accident to the insurance company if the accident is under $500.

10. You _____ contact a lawyer if you are hurt.

11. You _____ get a copy of the police report from the police station.

12. If the damage is not serious, you _____ try to settle the cost of the damages without calling the police or the insurance company.

Write a short description of an accident you were involved in or an accident you witnessed.

DESCRIPTION OF ACCIDENT
OFFICER'S SIGNATURE _____

Role play

With two other students, write and practice a conversation at the scene of an accident. One student is a police officer and the other two students are drivers who just had an accident. Tell the officer what happened. Present your conversation to the class.

6 Thank You I'm Sorry

Discuss

Have you done a favor for someone lately? What did you do?
Have you apologized to someone recently? What did you say?

Read

In every country it is important to thank other people for favors, both large and small ones. Many people feel that the words "Thank you" are the most important words in the English language. Most Americans think that both children and older people should be thanked for any kind act. The person accepting the thanks usually says, "It was a pleasure to help you," or simply, "You're welcome." If a person is the recipient of a gift or special favor, Americans sometimes send a thank-you card with a simple message.

It is equally important to apologize when you have hurt or disappointed someone. When possible, it is nice to add an explanation or excuse for the behavior. People who are late often blame traffic jams or accidents that stopped traffic. A person who was grouchy on Monday and had an argument may apologize on Tuesday saying, "Sorry I lost my temper yesterday. I haven't been feeling well lately."

If someone breaks, loses, or damages another person's property, he should apologize and offer to pay for the item. Most of the time, the other person accepts the apology graciously and may not show any disappointment or anger. But if the problem was serious or it happened several times before, the person might say something to show how he feels. You might say that thank yous and apologies are the oil that keep the world moving smoothly.

Read each sentence. If it is true, write T. If it is false, write F.

_____ 1. It is only necessary to thank a person who is older than you.

_____ 2. If your friend lends you his car for a morning, you should send him a thank-you card.

_____ 3. When you apologize for something, try to explain the reason for your actions.

_____ 4. When someone apologizes to you, tell him how upset you are.

_____ 5. If you break a friend's camera, you should offer to buy her a new one.

Howard: Hi, June.
June: Hi, Howard. How's the car?
Howard: It's running fine now. It was just the battery. I want to thank you for driving me to work yesterday.
June: Don't mention it. It was no problem. I'm sorry I was a little late. The baby-sitter was a few minutes late.
Howard: That's all right. Thanks again.
June: Anytime.

Practice this model. Thank people for the following favors.

I want to thank you for	
Thanks for	***driving me to work*** .
I really appreciate your*	

* your—formal speech; you—informal speech

1. drive me to work

2. baby-sit for me yesterday

3. help me with my homework

4. pick up my son at school

5. watch my house last week

6. let me use your car

7. lend me this CD

8. help me clean up after the party

9. drive me to the store

Write four sentences thanking another student or a friend for doing a favor. Use one of these responses.

You're welcome.	It was no trouble at all.
Don't mention it.	No problem.
It was my pleasure.	Anytime.

1. A: Thanks for _____.
   B: _____.

2. A: I want to thank you for _____.
   B: _____.

3. A: I really appreciate you _____.
   B: _____.

4. A: I really appreciate your _____.
   B: _____.

Practice this model. Apologize and give an excuse.

A: I'm sorry I _____ **missed my appointment** _____.
   or
   I'm sorry about
   Please excuse me for _____ **missing my appointment** _____.
   I'd like to apologize for
   _____ **I was sick** _____.
B: Don't worry about it. It's all right.

1. miss my appointment
   I / be sick

2. be late
   My car / break down

3. break your camera
   It / slip out of my hand

4. lose my temper
   I / be very upset

5. hang up on you
   I / lose my temper

6. hurt your feelings
   I / be tired when
   I see you

Practice this model. Apologize and give an excuse.

A: I'm sorry I _____ **didn't return your call** _____.
    or
    I'm sorry about
    Please excuse me for _____ **not returning your call** _____.
    I'd like to apologize for
    _____ **I forgot all about it** _____.
B: Don't worry about it. It's all right.

1. not return your call   2. not write sooner   3. not send you a card

4. not pick you up   5. not come on time   6. not bring the
    yesterday   pictures

Apologize for your actions.

Partner Exercise

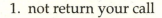

Student 1	**Student 2**
I'm sorry I / be late	*Listen carefully and help Student 1.*
I'm sorry I was late.	

Student 1

1. I'm sorry I / be late
2. I'm sorry for / be late
3. Please excuse me for / lose my temper.
4. I'm sorry I / lose my temper.
5. I'm sorry I / not come on time
6. I'd like to apologize for / not come on time
7. I'm sorry I / forget your birthday
8. I'm sorry about / forget your birthday
9. Please excuse me for / not call you
10. I'm sorry I / not call you

(FOLD HERE)

Student 2

1. I'm sorry I was late.
2. I'm sorry for being late.
3. Please excuse me for losing my temper.
4. I'm sorry I lost my temper.
5. I'm sorry I didn't come on time.
6. I'd like to apologize for not coming on time.
7. I'm sorry I forgot your birthday.
8. I'm sorry about forgetting your birthday.
9. Please excuse me for not calling you.
10. I'm sorry I didn't call you.

complete

Write five sentences apologizing to another student or a friend. Give an excuse for your actions. Use some of the excuses below or think of your own reasons.

> It slipped my mind.
>
> I just forgot all about it.
>
> I don't know where my head was.
>
> I was upset about something.

1.   A: I'm sorry about _____.
       B: _____.

2.   A: Please excuse me for not _____.
       B: _____.

3.   A: I'm sorry I _____.
       B: _____.

4.   A: I'm sorry I didn't _____.
       B: _____.

5.   A: I'd like to apologize for _____.
       B: _____.

Interaction

Ask two students these questions about a favor and an apology. Fill in their answers on the chart below.

	Student 1	Student 2
Have you done a favor for anyone recently? Please explain.		
Have you apologized to anyone recently? Please explain.		
What excuse did you give?		

Role play

Write and practice two conversations between friends. In the first, thank your friend for doing a favor. In the second, apologize for something you did and give an excuse. Present your dialogues to the class.

Read these two thank-you notes. Then, write two thank-you notes below. In the first, thank a friend for a gift you received. In the second, thank a friend for doing a special favor.

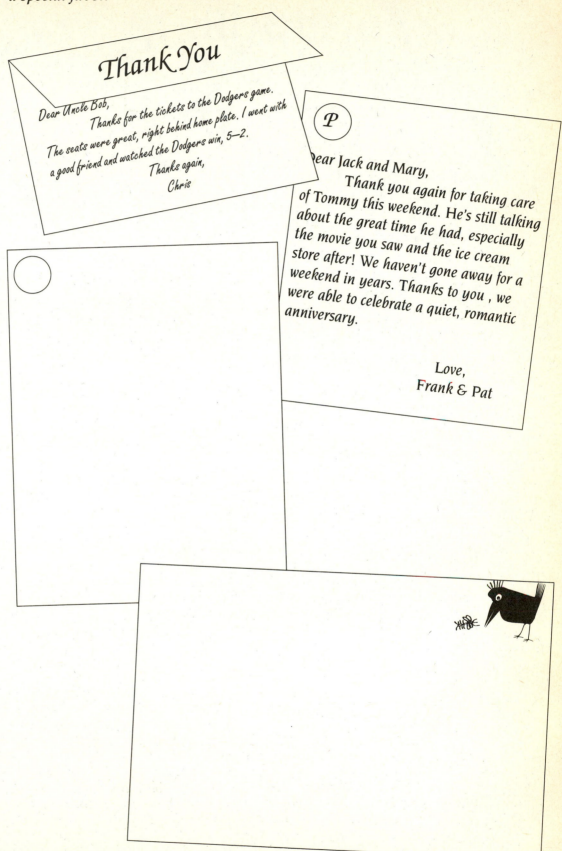

Thank You

Dear Uncle Bob,
   Thanks for the tickets to the Dodgers game. The seats were great, right behind home plate. I went with a good friend and watched the Dodgers win, 5–2.
   Thanks again,
   Chris

P

Dear Jack and Mary,
   Thank you again for taking care of Tommy this weekend. He's still talking about the great time he had, especially the movie you saw and the ice cream store after! We haven't gone away for a weekend in years. Thanks to you , we were able to celebrate a quiet, romantic anniversary.

   Love,
   Frank & Pat

7 Housing

Discuss

Do you rent an apartment or own a house?
Have you ever had a repair problem in your apartment? Explain the problem.
How long did it take the manager to correct the problem?

Read

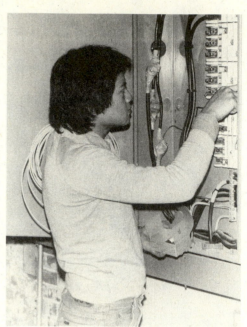

When you are having a problem in your apartment, you should notify the manager, superintendent, or landlord as soon as possible. It is best to talk to her and also give her a note explaining the problem. If the repairs are not made in a reasonable amount of time, send a second, stronger letter to her explaining the problem again. Remind her how long you have been waiting and say that you will "take other steps" if the repairs are not made by a specific date. It is important to keep a record of the dates when you speak to her and keep copies of letters that you have sent. If you need to send a third complaint letter, you should send it by certified mail.

If the landlord still doesn't make the repairs, you can often get help from a local government agency. Call the Housing Authority or Board of Health in your community and make a formal complaint against the landlord. They will usually send an inspector to check the problem, and they will contact the landlord and require her to make the necessary repairs.

Under very serious circumstances, you may be permitted to withhold a portion of the rent or fix the problem yourself and deduct the cost from the rent. However, before doing this, get legal advice from a lawyer or the Housing/Health Department in your area. If you stop paying the rent without following proper procedures, the landlord may try to evict you.

Read each sentence. If it is true, write T. If it is false, write F.

_____ 1 If the manager doesn't fix the problems in your apartment, you can stop paying the rent immediately.

_____ 2. If your stove is not working properly, call and write a note to the manager.

_____ 3. Send a strong complaint letter to the manager if the problem is not fixed in a reasonable amount of time.

_____ 4. You should usually fix a problem in your apartment by yourself and deduct the cost from the rent.

_____ 5. If the landlord will not fix a leaking pipe under your sink, you should contact the Housing Authority or Board of Health in your area.

Mrs. Sanchez: This is Mrs. Sanchez, Apartment 251. We've had a leak under the sink for a week. I've called you three times already.

Manager: Mrs. Sanchez, I've been very busy. I'll be up soon.

Mrs. Sanchez: That's what you said yesterday and this morning. If you don't fix it by 3:00, I'll have to take other action.

Manager: Don't worry, I'll be up.

Practice this model with the housing problems below.

This is ___(your name)___, Apartment ___5B___.

We've had _____a problem with the refrigerator_____ for ___three weeks___.

1. a problem with the
   refrigerator
   three weeks

3. a broken window
   in our bedroom
   a month

3. a leak in our
   kitchen ceiling
   five days

4. a problem with the
   stove
   two days

5. plaster falling from
   the bedroom ceiling
   a month

6. ants
   a few weeks

7. mice
   a month

8. rats
   a week

9. cockroaches
   two months

Practice this model with the housing problems below.

This is ___**(your name)**___, Apartment ___**215**___.
We haven't had _____**electricity**_____ since ___**this morning**___.

1. electricity
   this mornings

2. hot water
   Friday

3. heat
   7:00 A.M.

4. gas
   yesterday

5. a light in the hall
   last week

6. garbage collection
   last Monday

Describe these symptoms.

Partner Exercise

Student 1	Student 2
not / gas / two days We haven't had gas for two days.	**Listen carefully and help Student 1.**

Student 1	Student 2
1. not / gas / two days	1. We haven't had gas for two days.
2. mice / two months	2. We've had mice for two months.
3. not / electricity / this morning	3. We haven't had electricity since this morning.
4. not / water / 9:00 A.M.	4. We haven't had water since 9:00 A.M.
5. cockroaches / a month	5. We've had cockroaches for a month.
6. a problem with the stove / two weeks	6. We've had a problem with the stove for two weeks.
7. not / garbage collection / last week	7. We haven't had garbage collection since last week.
8. rats / week	8. We've had rats for a week.
9. not / heat / two days	9. We haven't had heat for two days.
10. a broken window / last Thursday	10. We've had a broken window since last Thursday.

(FOLD HERE)

44

Complete these conversations between a tenant and a manager.

Tenant: This is _____, Apartment _____ .

_____ mice for _____ .

I _____ already.

Manager: Don't _____ . I _____ come tomorrow morning

around _____ .

Tenant: This _____, Apartment _____.

I _____ since _____ .

I _____.

Manager: OK. I _____ later this afternoon.

Tenant: I_____ times already, so

please be sure to come this afternoon.

Manager: I _____ be there.

Interaction

Ask another student about a repair problem. Fill in the information on the chart below.

Do you live in a house or in an apartment?	
Do you have any repair problems in your home?	
How long have you had this problem?	
What have you done to fix this problem?	
Who have you called to fix this problem?	
What other problems have you had in the past?	

Match the problem with the repair person.

__b__ 1. fixes pipes

_____ 2. gets rid of mice

_____ 3. wallpapers a kitchen

_____ 4. repairs a refrigerator

_____ 5. puts in a new light fixture

_____ 6. installs kitchen cabinets

_____ 7. repairs a sidewalk

a. an electrician

b. a plumber

c. an exterminator

d. a mason

e. an appliance repair person

f. a painter

g. a carpenter

Complete this letter of complaint. Sign your name.

_____, _____

Dear Mr. Hollander,

We _____ for two weeks. I've

called you _____ times, but nothing has been done . Please call me

immediately to arrange a time to _____. If you don't

_____ by next week, I'll have to take further action.

Sincerely,

Apartment 2B

Write a letter of complaint asking the manager / landlord to fix a problem in your apartment or house. You have told the manager about this problem several times.

Laura has had a few problems in her apartment for two weeks. She's called the manager four times. Each time he promises to fix the problems, but he never comes. Describe some of the problems in Laura's bathroom.

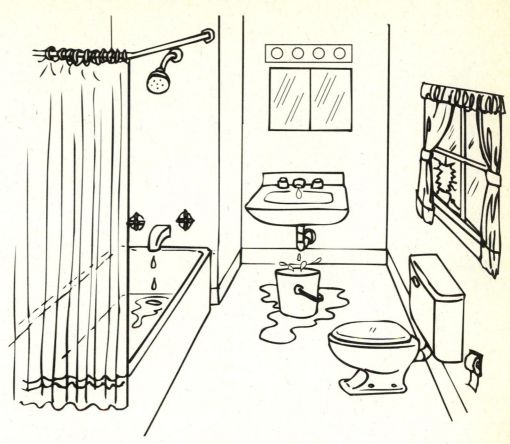

Sit in a small group. Based on the housing regulations or laws in your area, decide what Laura should do. Write "should" or "shouldn't" in the blank.

1. She _____ call the manager again.

2. She _____ write a letter to the manager.

3. If necessary, she _____ send a second letter by certified mail.

4. She _____ stop paying the rent immediately.

5. She _____ only pay a portion of the rent.

6. She _____ fix it herself.

7. She _____ call the Board of Health or Housing Department in her area.

8. She _____ contact a lawyer immediately.

9. She _____ pay a plumber and deduct the cost from her rent.

10. If necessary, she _____ go to court to get a rent reduction and fix the problems.

Role play

With another student, write and practice a conversation between a tenant and a manager / landlord. The tenant is upset because the manager has not fixed a problem in the apartment. Present your dialogue to the class.

8 A Medical Check Up

Discuss

Why is it important to have regular checkups?
Where do you and your family go for medical attention?
When you go to the doctor, do you usually understand the doctor's explanations and instructions?

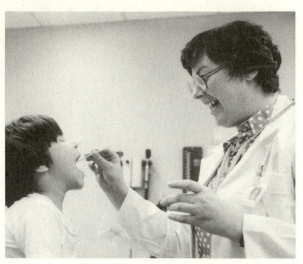

Read

Both children and adults need to practice preventative medicine to maintain healthy lifestyles and to detect medical problems early. Children need to see their pediatricians for regular checkups and for immunizations. Adults should see a general practitioner or internist to get a physical every year or two. As part of the exam, the doctor will check the heart and lungs and other organs and will usually take blood and urine samples to check for high cholesterol, anemia, high blood sugar, and any infections. Women should also see their gynecologists every year. Regular checkups can catch many problems, such as cancer, while they are still treatable.

When you see a doctor about a medical problem, the doctor will want you to describe your problem and your symptoms in detail. The doctor will check you and may want you to get extra tests in the office, at a lab, or at a local hospital. After the doctor has diagnosed your problem, feel free to ask questions so that you completely understand the problem, what caused it, and how the doctor wants to treat it.

If the doctor prescribes medicine to treat your problem, find out the purpose of the medicine , how to take it, and if it has any side effects. Be sure to tell the doctor if you are allergic to any medicines. You can ask the doctor or pharmacist if the drug is available in generic form, which may cost less than the same drug in a brand name.

Read each sentence. If it is true, write T. If it is false, write F.

_____ 1. Children need a series of immunizations from their pediatricians.

_____ 2. A man between the ages of 25 and 35 should get a checkup every five years.

_____ 3. If you don't understand what the doctor has told you, you should ask, "Could you explain that to me again?"

_____ 4. When the doctor gives you a prescription, you should ask, "What are the side effects of this medication?"

_____ 5. Generic drugs are usually more expensive than brand name drugs.

Doctor:	What seems to be the problem?
Mrs. Benin:	I've been nauseous for three days.
Doctor:	Any other problems?
Mrs. Benin:	I've been a little dizzy.
Doctor:	How long have you been dizzy?
Mrs. Benin:	Since Tuesday.

Practice this model and ask questions about the symptoms below.

I've been ___*very tired*___ for ___*a few weeks*___ .	___**She's**___ had ___*a rash*___ since ___*Monday*___ .

1. I /very tired/
   a few weeks

2. She /a rash/
   Monday

3. I /congested/
   four days

4. My son /a sore throat/
   Thursday

5. I /depressed/
   a month

6. My son/a fever/
   yesterday

7. My daughter/sick/
   a few days

8. I /a backache/
   last week

9. My daughter/nauseous/
   two days

10. My son/constipated/
    five days

11. I /a cough/
    Wednesday

12. I /stomach cramps/
    last weekend

Describe these symptoms.

Partner Exercise

Student 1

I / backache / two days
I've had a backache for two days.

1. I / a backache / two days
2. I / very tired / a week
3. My son / a fever / Sunday
4. My daughter / constipated / three days.
5. I / stomach cramps / Monday
6. My son / a rash / a few days
7. I / dizzy / Thursday
8. My daughter / a cough / four days
9. I / a sore throat / a week
10. My son / congested / last week

(FOLD HERE)

Student 2

Listen carefully and help Student 1.

1. I've had a backache for two days.
2. I've been very tired for a week.
3. My son's had a fever since Sunday.
4. My daughter's been constipated for three days.
5. I've had stomach cramps since Monday.
6. My son's had a rash for a few days.
7. I've been dizzy since Thursday.
8. My daughter's had a cough for four days.
9. I've had a sore throat for a week.
10. My son's been congested since last week.

Practice this model and ask questions about the symptoms below.

A: How long ___*have you*___ ___*been congested*___ ?
B: ___*Since Friday*___ .

A: How long ___*has she*___ ___*had a rash*___ ?
B: ___*For three days*___ .

1. you / congested?
   Friday

2. she / a rash?
   three days

3. you / a headache?
   Sunday

4. he / nauseous?
   two days

5. daughter / diarrhea?
   Tuesday

6. you / short of breath?
   a week

Partner Exercise

Ask questions with How long.

Student 1

you / backache?
How long have you had a backache?

1. you / a backache?
2. he / headache?
3. she / nauseous?
4. you / depressed?
5. you / short of breath?
6. he / constipated?
7. she / a cough?
8. she / a fever?
9. you / stomach cramps?
10. he / congested?

(FOLD HERE)

Student 2
Listen carefully and help Student 1.

1. How long have you had a backache?
2. How long has he had a headache?
3. How long has she been nauseous?
4. How long have you been depressed?
5. How long have you been short of breath?
6. How long has he been constipated?
7. How long has she had a cough?
8. How long has she had a fever?
9. How long have you had stomach cramps?
10. How long has he been congested?

complete

Complete these conversations between a doctor and a patient.

Sofia:	I've been _____.
Doctor:	How long have you _____?
Sofia:	For _____.
Doctor:	Any other problems?
Sofia:	Yes, I've had a _____.
Doctor:	How long have you _____?
Sofia:	Since _____.

Hoang:	I've been _____.
Doctor:	How long have you _____?
Hoang:	For _____.
Doctor:	Any other problems?
Hoang:	Yes, I've had a _____.
Doctor:	How long have you _____?
Hoang:	Since _____.

Ed:	I've been _____.
Doctor:	How long have you _____?
Ed:	For _____.
Doctor:	Any other problems?
Ed:	Yes, I've had a _____.
Doctor:	How long have you _____?
Ed:	Since _____.

David is six years old. He has the chicken pox. Talk about David's symptoms. How does he feel?

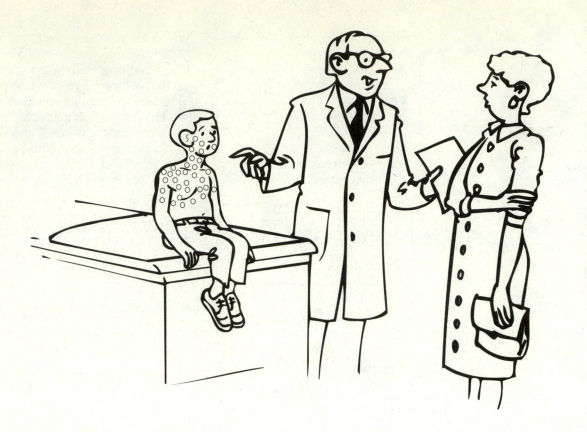

These are some questions that a parent should ask the doctor about a child's illness. Discuss these questions about David's illness with your teacher.

1. What does he have?
2. Is it contagious?
3. How long will he be sick?
4. Does he have to stay home from school?
5. When can he go back to school?
6. What are you prescribing?
7. What does the medicine do?
8. Are there any side effects from the medication?
9. How often should I give him the medication?
10. What else should I do?

Role play

With another student, write and practice a conversation between a parent and a pediatrician. The parent will describe the child's symptoms and the doctor will diagnose the problem. The parent will then ask several questions about the child's illness. Present your dialogue to the class.

You are starting to feel sick. Sit in a small group and talk about what home remedies and over-the-counter drugs you could use to take care of yourself in each situation.

I have a headache.	I have a low fever.
1. **You could take an aspirin.**	1. _____
2. _____	2. _____
3. _____	3. _____

I have a stomachache.	I am constipated.
1. _____	1. _____
2. _____	2. _____
3. _____	3. _____

I am depressed.	I am congested.
1. _____	1. _____
2. _____	2. _____
3. _____	3. _____

Go Find Out

Joe hasn't been feeling well. He's had a cough for three weeks and now he's very tired and has a fever. Joe doesn't have enough money to see a doctor or to pay for a prescription. If Joe lived in your area, how could he get proper medical care? What clinics, hospital services, or other medical services are available free of charge or for reduced payment?

_____

_____

_____

_____

_____

9 Medical History

Discuss

What do you do when medical symptoms persist for a few days?
What kinds of medical tests have you or a member of your family had?
What kinds of questions are on a medical history form?

Read

When you do not feel well for a long time or have a persistent problem, it is important to go to a doctor and check out your symptoms. To help in diagnosing a problem, a doctor generally will perform a physical examination, may request tests, and will review your medical history.

The first time you see a doctor, you usually have to fill out a medical history form. This form asks for medical information about you, your parents, and other family members and whether you or they have had diseases such as cancer, heart disease, or diabetes. Additionally, the form usually asks about immunizations for diseases such as polio, tetanus, measles, or mumps. It will ask about continuing medical problems, medications you take regularly, and allergies. The doctor may want to know about your lifestyle, including smoking, drinking, stress, and the amount of exercise you get.

In addition to the information the doctor gets from your exam and from any tests, she will review your medical history in making a diagnosis. Your lifestyle or your family's medical history may indicate special risk factors. Certain illnesses such as diabetes, heart disease, and cancer run in families. That means that persons in those families are at a greater risk of getting those illnesses. For example, if your medical history indicates that two people in your family have diabetes, the doctor may monitor you for this even though you show no symptoms.

Read each sentence. If it is true, write T. If it is false, write F.

_____ 1. Each time you visit a doctor, you will have to fill out a medical history form.

_____ 2. You should see a doctor if you have had a pain in your stomach for two weeks.

_____ 3. It is helpful for the doctor to know if you are going through a stressful situation, such as a divorce.

_____ 4. If your medical history form shows that your father had cancer, the doctor will monitor you for this problem.

_____ 5. If both a mother and a father both have diabetes, the children will always develop diabetes, too.

54

Listen, Read and Say

Doctor:	What's the problem?
Carmen:	I've had a terrible headache for three days.
Doctor:	Have you had these headaches before?
Carmen:	No, I haven't.
Doctor:	Have you been under any pressure recently?
Carmen:	Not that I know of.
Doctor:	Have you seen an eye doctor lately?
Carmen:	Yes, I saw one three months ago.
Doctor:	We'll need to do some further tests.

Practice this model. **Ask questions about the symptoms below**

Have you been under any pressure _____?

Yes, **I have.**   or   No, **I haven't**.

1. I've had a terrible headache for five days.
   a. you / be under any pressure?
   b. you / have these headaches before?
   c. you / see an eye doctor recently?

2. My son's had a rash since Saturday.
   a. he / have this before?
   b. he / eat anything different lately?
   c. he / have any allergies?
   d. you / change your family's soap or detergent?

3. I've had a backache since Monday.
   a. you / have this before?
   b. you / lift anything heavy?
   c. you / fall recently?
   d. you / have a cold recently?

4. My daughter's been nauseous for three days.
   a. she / eat anything different recently?
   b. she / have regular bowel movements?
   c. she / have stomach cramps?
   d. she / lose any weight lately?

Partner Exercise

Ask these questions about a patient's symptoms

<table>
<tr><td align="center">Student 1</td><td></td><td align="center">Student 2</td></tr>
<tr><td>you / eat anything different lately?</td><td></td><td>Listen carefully and help Student 1.</td></tr>
<tr><td>Have you eaten anything different lately?</td><td></td><td></td></tr>
</table>

Student 1	Student 2
1. you / eat anything different lately?	1. Have you eaten anything different lately?
2. he / take any medication recently?	2. Has he taken any medication recently?
3. she / feel this way before?	3. Has she felt this way before?
4. you / be under any pressure?	4. Have you been under any pressure?
5. he / be nauseous?	5. Has he been nauseous?
6. she / have any chest pains?	6. Has she had any chest pains?
7. you / lift anything heavy?	7. Have you lifted anything heavy?
8. she / change her lifestyle recently?	8. Has she changed her lifestyle recently?
9. he / fall recently?	9. Has he fallen recently?
10. you / have regular bowel movements lately?	10. Have you had regular bowel movements lately?

(FOLD HERE)

Practice

Practice this model with the symptoms below.

A: _____**Have you lost any weight lately**_____?

B: Yes, _____**I lost twenty pounds last month.**_____

1.   I've been very tired for a month.

| lose any weight lately? | Yes / lose twenty pounds last month |
| change your lifestyle? | Yes / get a part-time job a few weeks ago |

2.   My son's had backache since Tuesday.

| lift anything heavy recently? | Yes / help a friend move last week |
| take any medication for the pain? | Yes / take some pain killers yesterday |

3.   My daughter's had a rash for two days.

| eat anything different lately? | Yes / eat some strawberries two days ago |
| have this before? | Yes / have a similar rash last summer |

4.  I've had a pain in my knee since Monday.

fall recently?   Yes / fall on my sidewalk two days ago

have a problem with your knee before?   Yes / twist it last year

5.  My son's been nauseous for three days.

have a fever?   Yes / have a 101° fever last night

vomit?   Yes / throw up yesterday afternoon

6. I've been depressed for three weeks.

be under any pressure lately?   Yes / lose my job last month

feel this way before?   Yes / be depressed two years ago

 *Work in a group of three students. Write two questions and answers for each of these medical problems.*

1. I've had a stomachache for a week.

   _____? _____.

   _____? _____.

2. I've had a pain in my shoulder for two days.

   _____? _____.

   _____? _____.

3. My son's been depressed for two months.

   _____? _____.

   _____? _____.

Lauri Johnson completed this Medical History Form. Discuss the purpose of each test and immunization below. Talk about any new vocabulary.

FAMILY HISTORY

Check any illnesses you, your parents or any siblings have had.

	Allergies	Anemia	Asthma	Diabetes	Cancer or Tumors	Epilepsy	Glaucoma	Alcoholism	Kidney Trouble	Stomach Problems	Nervous breakdown	Arthritis	High Blood Pressure	Heart Trouble
Father					✔								✔	
Mother				✔								✔		✔
Sibling(s)			✔		✔			✔						
Self	✔									✔		✔		

Hospitalizations

List any major medical illnesses or operations.

Year	Operation
1991	*Knee surgery*
1994	*appendicitis*

Tests and Immunizations

Check all tests and immunizations you have had. Write the year of the most recent immunization.

chest x-ray	19 91	MRI	19 ___	tetanus shot	19 85
EKG	19 ___	mammogram	19 94	polio series	19 63
biopsy	19 ___	TB test	19 ___	typhoid shot	19 64
G.I. series	19 92	___	19 ___	MMR shot	19 64
PAP smear	19 93	___	19 ___	flu shot	19 95

Medications

Check any medications you are taking now. Circle any medications you are allergic to.

- ☐ antibiotics
- ☐ (penicillin)
- ☐ sulfa
- ☐ codeine
- ☐ sedatives
- ☐ stimulants
- ☐ Demerol
- ☑ cold tablets
- ☐ diuretics
- ☑ aspirin
- ☐ antacids
- ☐ laxatives
- ☐ blood pressure medication
- ☐ _____
- ☐ _____
- ☐ _____

In a small group, discuss these questions about Lauri Johnson's medical history.

1. Is there a history of any disease in Lauri's family?
2. Has Lauri ever been in the hospital?
3. Has she ever had an operation?
4. Has Lauri ever had a chest x-ray? When?
5. Has she ever had a G.I. series? When?
6. Has she ever had a mammogram? When?
7. Has Lauri had a recent tetanus shot?
8. Has she had her polio series?
9. What medications is she currently taking?
10. Is she allergic to any medication?

The following are some common questions that are found on a Medical History Form. Discuss the new vocabulary, then answer the questions about your medical history.

MEDICAL HISTORY FORM

1.	Do you have any skin problems?	Yes	No
2.	Does your skin ever itch or burn?	Yes	No
3.	Have you ever had seizures or convulsions?	Yes	No
4.	Do you get nosebleeds?	Yes	No
5.	Have you gained or lost more than ten pounds in the last six months?	Yes	No
6.	Are you tired or exhausted most of the time?	Yes	No
7.	Do you exercise three times a week or more?	Yes	No
8.	Are your joints ever swollen?	Yes	No
9.	Do you ever have pain in your back or shoulders?	Yes	No
10.	Do you smoke?	Yes	No
11.	Do you have two or more alcoholic drinks a day?	Yes	No
12.	Do you use sleeping pills, marijuana, tranquilizers or pain killers?	Yes	No
13.	Do you often have heartburn?	Yes	No
14.	Have you ever vomited blood?	Yes	No
15.	Are your bowel movements ever black or bloody?	Yes	No
16.	Have you ever had burning when you urinate?	Yes	No
17.	Do you have a constant feeling that you have to urinate?	Yes	No
18.	Have you had trouble with your eyes in the past year?	Yes	No
19.	Do you have any difficulty hearing?	Yes	No
20.	Is your nose stuffed up when you don't have a cold?	Yes	No
21.	Do you sometimes wheeze or gasp for air?	Yes	No
22.	Do you have high blood pressure?	Yes	No
23.	Do you ever get pains in your chest?	Yes	No
24.	Do you ever feel dizzy or lightheaded?	Yes	No
25.	Are you ever short of breath?	Yes	No

For women only:

1.	What was the date of your last period?	_____	
2.	Do you have heavy bleeding with your periods?	Yes	No
3.	Do you ever have bleeding between your periods?	Yes	No
4.	Do you examine your breasts at least once a month?	Yes	No
5.	Do you have any lumps or pain in your breasts?	Yes	No

10 College Choices

Discuss

What public and private colleges are in your area?

What can you study at these colleges?

Do any relatives or friends attend these colleges?

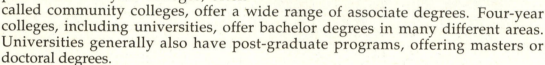

complete

Today in the United States there is a college for just about everyone. Students can attend either two-year or four-year public or private colleges and can study full time or part time. Two-year colleges, often called community colleges, offer a wide range of associate degrees. Four-year colleges, including universities, offer bachelor degrees in many different areas. Universities generally also have post-graduate programs, offering masters or doctoral degrees.

Students can often get financial aid and scholarships to help pay for tuition. Financial aid is usually based on family income, but scholarships are based on a student's academic or athletic ability. An excellent student who does not have much money can usually get an aid package which might include scholarships, financial aid grants, loans, and student work-study to pay for college tuition. Tuition at public colleges is much less than tuition at private colleges.

Admission standards at both public and private colleges vary greatly. Some of the best colleges in the United States are public. Many community colleges have open admissions, that is, they accept all students. Four-year private and public college admission standards range from easy to extremely competitive. Admissions offices analyze grades from high school and scores on standardized tests such as the SAT (Scholastic Aptitude Test), the ACT (American College Test), and the TOEFL (Test of English as a Foreign Language). They also consider the student's extracurricular activities, including sports, clubs, and leadership positions while in high school.

Read each sentence. If it is true, write T. If it is false, write F.

_____ 1. Public colleges usually cost less than private colleges.

_____ 2. Public colleges offer an excellent education.

_____ 3. Some colleges are more difficult to get into than other colleges.

_____ 4. If a family's income is low, a student can still attend college.

_____ 5. You can get a bachelor's degree in psychology at a two-year college.

Listen, Read and Say

Mark: I'm applying to Hart College.
Amy: That's a good college.
Mark: Yeah. I'd like to major in business, maybe in accounting.
Amy: Have you sent in your application yet?
Mark: No. I've already filled out the application, but I haven't written the essay yet.
Amy: Well, good luck.

Practice this model with the steps in the college application process.

I've	*filled out the application* already.
	already *filled out the application*.
I haven't	*filled out the application* yet.

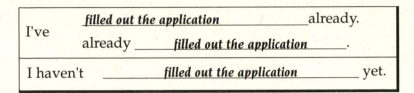

1. fill out the application

2. take the SAT / ACT / TOEFL

3. write an essay

4. send my high school transcript

5. get two letters of recommendation

6. apply for financial aid

7. visit the school

8. go for an interview

9. apply for a scholarship

UNION COMMUNITY COLLEGE 2-year college Florida Men: 6,000 Women: 5,000 Tuition $2,400 87% of students receive financial aid Test scores: Open admissions Application deadline: March 1	**WESTERN TECHNICAL COLLEGE** 2-year technical college Colorado Men: 2,000 Women: 1,100 Tuition $4,000 Rm and Brd $3,100 82% of students receive financial aid Test scores: Average Application deadline: January 15
WESTON STATE COLLEGE Arizona Men: 2,700 Women: 3,300 Tuition $6,000 Rm and Brd $4,000 82% of students receive financial aid Test scores: Average Application deadline: February 1	**CARLTON STATE COLLEGE** Illinois Men: 9,000 Women: 10,000 Tuition $4,000 state residents / $7,000 out-of-state residents Rm and Brd $5,000 87% of students receive financial aid Test scores: Well above average Application deadline: December 30
DRAKE COLLEGE Pennsylvania Men: 750 Women: 900 Tuition $13,000 Rm and Brd $6,500 70% of students receive financial aid Test scores: Above average Application deadline: December 1	**BARKER UNIVERSITY** Michigan Men: 9,100 Women: 9,700 Tuition $15,000 Rm and Brd $7,000 75% of students receive financial aid Test scores: Average Application deadline: January 1

Practice the model and talk about these six colleges.

This college is located in _____.

It's a two-year / four-year college.

The enrollment is _____ men and _____ women.

The tuition is _____. Room and board is _____.

About _____% of the students receive some kind of financial aid.

The test scores are _____.

The application deadline is _____.

Complete this information. Compare Drake College and Carlton State College.

DRAKE COLLEGE	CARLTON STATE COLLEGE
Pennsylvania Men: 750 Women: 900 Tuition $13,000 Rm and Brd $6,500 70% of students receive financial aid Test scores: Above average Application deadline: December 1	Illinois Men: 9,000 Women: 10,000 Tuition $4,000 state residents / $7,000 out of state residents Rm and Brd $5,000 87% of students receive financial aid Test scores: Well above average Application deadline: December 30

1. _____ is larger than _____.

2. _____ is smaller than _____.

3. _____ is closer to here than _____.

4. _____ is farther from here than _____.

5. _____ is more expensive than _____.

6. _____ is less expensive than _____.

7. _____ is more competitive than _____.

8. _____ is less competitive than _____.

Interaction

Ask another student about a family member or friend in college. Fill in the information on the chart below.

Do you know anyone who is attending college?	
Where does she go?	
Where is it located?	
Does she live at college or does she commute?	
How big is the college?	
What is she majoring in?	
What year is she in?	
What is the tuition?	
Does she work part-time?	
How does she like the college?	

Joseph is a high school senior. His high school grades are mostly Bs, with As in math. He wants to go to college and major in computer science. Joseph applied to five colleges and was accepted by three.

Joseph is one of three children. His parents earn $34,000 a year. They would like Joseph to go to college, but they have not been able to save any money. Joseph has received financial aid packages from each of the schools.

	Simpson Community College	Hart State College	Southern College
Type	2-year community college	4-year public college	4-year private college
Location	15 miles from home	80 miles from home	200 miles from home
Enrollment	10,000	18,000	3,000
Living Arrangements	live at home/commute by car	live in dorm on campus	live in dorm on campus
Tuition (plus room and board)	$2,500	$11,000	$21,000
Financial aid package	aid: $2,500	aid: $5,000 loan: $3,000 work-study: $1,000	aid: $10,000 loan: $5,000 work-study: $2,000

Sit in a small group and discuss these questions.

1. Is Joseph a serious student?
2. What does he want to major in?
3. Which school is the closest to home?
4. Which school is the most expensive?
5. How much more money do Joseph and his parents need for each school?
6. Would Joseph need a car to attend any of the schools?
7. How much will Joseph owe in loans after four years at each college?
8. What are some advantages and disadvantages of each school?

Which school should Joseph choose? If the school is more expensive than the financial aid, where could he get the additional money?

Go **Find Out**

In your local or school library, you can find many college catalogs. Research the following information on four colleges in your state. Complete the information on the chart below. As a group, discuss different colleges in your state. Then, write five sentences comparing some of the colleges.

Name: _____

Location: _____

Circle one: Two-year   Four-year

Circle one: Public   Private

Enrollment: _____

Tuition: _____

Room and Board: _____

Required tests: SAT ACT   TOEFL

Test scores: _____

Application deadline: _____

Other: _____

_____

Name: _____

Location: _____

Circle one: Two-year   Four-year

Circle one: Public   Private

Enrollment: _____

Tuition: _____

Room and Board: _____

Required tests: SAT ACT   TOEFL

Test scores: _____

Application deadline: _____

Other: _____

_____

Name: _____

Location: _____

Circle one: Two-year   Four-year

Circle one: Public   Private

Enrollment: _____

Tuition: _____

Room and Board: _____

Required tests: SAT ACT   TOEFL

Test scores: _____

Application deadline: _____

Other: _____

_____

Name: _____

Location: _____

Circle one: Two-year   Four-year

Circle one: Public   Private

Enrollment: _____

Tuition: _____

Room and Board: _____

Required tests: SAT ACT   TOEFL

Test scores: _____

Application deadline: _____

Other: _____

_____

1. _____

2. _____

3. _____

4. _____

5. _____

11 Community Resources

Discuss

What kinds of personal problems do individuals and families sometimes have?

How do these problems affect individuals and families?

Who can people talk with when they are having problems with their children?

Read

In our complicated world many people, at some point in their lives, suffer life crises and need temporary help for themselves or for someone in their family. For many years, there were few places people could go for help or counseling, but now people can contact various public and private agencies who are interested in listening and helping people to find solutions. These agencies provide immediate crisis intervention and longer term counseling.

Too often, people are reluctant to seek outside help. They want to feel independent and to handle their own problems. However, when a problem keeps escalating, it is important to contact professional help to find ways to improve the situation before it is out of control. For example, consider a wife who has been getting more and more scared because her husband is jealous and has been threatening her whenever she goes out of the house. He has been pushing her, but has not yet struck her. Now is the time to contact a counseling agency, before the problem gets worse.

To get advice or assistance with personal, family, alcohol and drug, housing or other problems, a person can easily contact an appropriate agency directly or through a local hotline number. The local hotline numbers are listed in telephone directories. A counselor will listen to your situation, and will counsel you or refer you to the agency or organization which can help you. This assistance is always confidential. If money is a problem, the counselor will assist you in finding low-cost help.

Read each sentence. If it is true, write T. If it is false, write F.

_____ 1. It is difficult to find a counselor to speak with when you have a crisis in your family.

_____ 2. If you don't face an abuse problem, the abuse usually gets worse as time goes on.

_____ 3. When you call a hotline number, you can speak to a counselor about your problem.

_____ 4. Hotline counselors provide long-term counseling.

_____ 5. You can get counseling services from local agencies even if your income is low.

Oscar: My brother goes out drinking all weekend and drinks at home almost every evening. Sometimes he gets violent. I'm worried about him and I don't know what to do.

Ana: Sounds like your brother has a drinking problem. Why don't you get him to call the Alcoholism Hotline?

Oscar: What would they do for him?

Ana: They'd listen and talk to him about his problems. And they'd tell him about Alcoholics Anonymous and other agencies in the area that could help him.

Oscar: I'm going to give him the number. I hope he calls. He's getting worse.

Practice this model with the problems below.

A: How would a/an _____ **General Crisis Hotline** _____ help someone?

B: They would **talk to someone about a problem** _____ .

1. General Crisis Hotline
   - talk to the person about a problem
   - refer the person to an agency for help
2. Alcoholism Agency
   - help the person stop drinking
   - provide counseling to the person and the family
3. Child Welfare Agency
   - provide counseling
   - investigate an abusive situation
   - take legal action
   - provide shelter for a child
4. Runaway Agency
   - provide counseling to a teenage runaway
   - provide shelter for a teenage runaway
5. Legal Aid Agency
   - give legal advice
   - tell the person his legal rights
   - represent a person in court
6. Housing Agency
   - give legal advice
   - require a landlord to make repairs
   - require a landlord to provide heat and hot water
7. Poison Control Hotline
   - tell the caller how to treat someone who took poison

complete

Read each problem. Then put the letter(s) of the hotline you would call for the following problems.

A. Alcoholism Hotline
B. Battered Women Hotline
C. Child Welfare Hotline
D. Consumer Hotline
E. Drug Abuse Hotline
F. Gamblers Anonymous Hotline

G. Mental Health Crisis Hotline
H. Housing Hotline
I. Legal Services Hotline
J. Poison Control Hotline
K. Rape Hotline
L. Runaway Hotline

___E___ 1. Your brother has started to use drugs.

_____ 2. You haven't had any heat in your apartment for two days.

_____ 3. Your spouse or parent threatens to hit you and you've been feeling more and more scared.

_____ 4. Your sister has been going out drinking most nights and has been taking a lot of sick days from work.

_____ 5. You need legal advice, but you don't have enough money for a lawyer.

_____ 6. You've been gambling a lot lately and you are more and more in debt.

_____ 7. A teenage relative has run away from home and needs to talk to someone.

_____ 8. Your child has just drunk some household cleaner.

_____ 9. You've been sleeping during the day and you've had difficulty getting yourself to go to work.

_____ 10. Your sister was just raped on her way home from work.

_____ 11. You bought an item in a store last month and it doesn't work. The store will not let you return or exchange the item.

_____ 12. Your neighbor has been leaving her children home alone at night while she works.

_____ 13. My son has been drinking on weekends and has been having problems at school.

_____ 14. My sister's husband left her with three children. She often starts crying and shaking and can't calm down. She's under extreme stress.

Practice this model with the following problems.

A: _**My friend has been drinking herself to sleep**_____.
I don't know what to do.
B: Why don't you call the _____**Alcoholism**_____ Hotline?

1. My friend / drink herself to sleep

2. My brother / use drugs

3. My neighbor / leave his child alone every morning

4. My neighbor / abuse his wife

5. I / feel very depressed

6. My son / gamble and lose a lot of money

7. My nephew / talk about committing suicide

8. My niece / threaten to run away

9. I / have a problem with the heat in my apartment

Read the situation below. Then sit in a small group and discuss the questions.

Bob is married and has three children. He was laid off from work six months ago. Since then, he hasn't been able to find a job. Before he got laid off, Bob drank a six pack of beer every evening. Lately, he's been drinking a lot more. Bob starts drinking in the early afternoon. By the evening, he's loud and gets angry at his wife, Sharon, and children for no reason. Dinner is unpleasant; Bob shouts at the children and complains that they are lazy and noisy. After dinner, Bob falls asleep in front of the TV set.

Everyone in the family has been affected by Bob's drinking. The children are not doing well in school and their grades are falling. Sharon's nerves are shot. She wonders if she still loves Bob.

1. What is Bob's problem?
2. Has he always had a drinking problem?
3. Why do you think he was laid off?
4. How has it affected his family?
5. Do you think that Bob believes he has a drinking problem?
6. What would an Alcoholism Hotline do for him?
7. If he will not seek help, what could Sharon do?
8. What else could the family do?

_____

_____

_____

Read the situation below. Then sit in a small group and write two or three suggestions for each question.

A family member has been depressed for several weeks. She is apathetic and has lost interest in work, family, food, and school. Whenever anything goes wrong, she blames herself. She'll wake up at 4:00 or 5:00 A.M. and will not be able to get back to sleep again. Recently, she's been having difficulty talking or concentrating. No one knows what to do.

How could you help this person?

_____

_____

_____

How could this person help herself or get help for herself?

_____

_____

_____

Look in the front of your local telephone book. Fill in the telephone numbers for these hotlines. If you do not find the number listed in your telephone book, try the information operator. You can also find the information in the library.

1. Alcoholism   _____
2. Drug Abuse   _____
3. Legal Services   _____
4. Gambling   _____
5. Rape   _____
6. Runaways   _____
7. Battered Women   _____
8. Child Abuse   _____
9. Poison Control   _____
10. Housing   _____
11. General Help / Crisis   _____
12. Consumer   _____
13. Police   _____
14. Fire Department   _____
15. Ambulance   _____

12 The Job Interview

What do you do for work now?
What other jobs have you had here and in your country?
Have you ever gone on a job interview? What happened?

Read

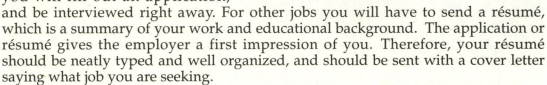

Finding a job can be a long process. Don't get discouraged. Applying and interviewing for jobs get easier with experience. Here are some tips.

When you apply for some jobs, you will fill out an application, and be interviewed right away. For other jobs you will have to send a résumé, which is a summary of your work and educational background. The application or résumé gives the employer a first impression of you. Therefore, your résumé should be neatly typed and well organized, and should be sent with a cover letter saying what job you are seeking.

At a job interview, the employer will try to find out what kind of person you are, what experience you have had, and how you can fit into the job situation. Before you go on an interview, practice explaining how your experience, skills, and abilities can help the company. It is good to ask some general questions about job responsibilities. It is better to wait until a job is offered before you ask specific questions about salary and benefits.

Always go to interviews alone. Wear neat, appropriate clothing. Try to arrive about ten minutes early. When you meet the interviewer, introduce yourself and shake hands. During the interview, look directly at the interviewer and answer the questions as specifically as you can. At the close of the interview, express your thanks and shake hands again.

Read each sentence. If it is true, write T. If it is false, write F.

_____ 1. If you type your résumé, it will usually make a better impression.

_____ 2. Résumés should only include information about job experience in this country.

_____ 3. It is best to wear business-style clothing for an interview.

_____ 4. At the interview, you can ask, "How many people will I be working with?"

_____ 5. At the interview, always get specific information about how many vacation days you will have.

Listen, Read and Say

Mrs. Fred Guzman is a mechanic and supervisor at Forest Auto Service. He is applying for the position of manager at the Bayville Auto Center. Ronald Green, the owner of Bayville Auto Center, is interviewing him now.

Mr. Green:	I was impressed with your résumé . You have several years experience in repairing cars and in supervision. How large an operation is Forest Auto Service?
Mr. Guzman:	It's a small operation. We have two bays and four mechanics. I'm in charge of scheduling and supervising. I do computer diagnostics, electrical repairs, and check all major work. We work with both foreign and domestic cars.
Mr. Green:	How long have you been there?
Mr. Guzman:	I began in 1992 as a mechanic. I've been supervisor for the last two years.
Mr. Green:	Are you ASE certified?
Mr. Guzman:	Yes, in most areas. I still need to take the test for heating and air conditioning.
Mr. Green:	What other jobs have you had?
Mr. Guzman:	Before this I worked at a plastics factory. I repaired the production machinery and made all the electrical repairs. Basically, I was in charge of maintaining and repairing every piece of equipment in the plant.
Mr. Green:	And you worked there for three years?
Mr. Guzman:	Yes. And on the weekends I was repairing and rebuilding car engines.
Mr. Green:	Tell me about your education.
Mr. Guzman:	I graduated from high school in Colombia in 1985. After high school, I attended a university for one year and studied engineering.
Mr. Green:	If I spoke with your employer, what would he tell me about you?
Mr. Guzman:	He'd say that I'm hardworking. I'm the first one there in the morning and I don't leave until the shop is in order. And I work well with the mechanics. I assign the work fairly and help out with difficult repairs.
Mr. Green:	Why are you looking to change jobs?
Mr. Guzman:	I like my current job, but we're a small shop. I'm ready to take on a bigger operation.
Mr. Green:	Well, thanks for coming in today. I'll call you in a few days.
Mr. Guzman:	Thank you.

Fred Guzman
65 Baker Street
San Francisco, California
(213) 789-3015

Objective: To manage an auto repair shop

Experience:

1992–Present *Mechanic.* Forest Auto Service, 346 Mission Street, San Francisco, California. Supervise auto repairs; diagnose and make repairs; check work; submit bills; have experience with both American and foreign cars.

1989–1992 *Maintenance Mechanic.* A&R Plastics, Inc., 32 Pueblo Drive, Los Angeles, California. Repaired all production machinery; made all electrical repairs; did general maintenance.

1987–1989 *Superintendent.* Buena Vista Apartments, Cali, Colombia. Complete charge of fifty apartments; repaired all plumbing; did carpentry work, painting and landscaping; assisted in all electrical work.

Education:

Present Alemany Community College, San Francisco, California. Studying English, advanced level.

1985–1987 Attended Universidad del Valle, Cali, Colombia. Completed one year of engineering courses.

1985 Graduated from high school, Cali, Colombia.

Special skills Experience in computerized billing
Bilingual - English and Spanish

References available upon request

Practice this information with the information from the résumé above.

Practice
Practice

Is he working now?
Exactly what does he do?
How long has he been there?
What other jobs has he had?
How long was he at each one?
Talk about his education.
Does he have any special skills?

Write a description of your present job:

Name of company _____

Address _____

Job duties _____

_____

_____

_____

Write a description of jobs you have had in the past:

Name of company _____

Address _____

Job duties _____

_____

_____

_____

Name of company _____

Address _____

Job duties _____

_____

_____

_____

Write a description of your educational background:

_____–Present _____

_____

_____–_____ _____

_____

_____–_____ _____

_____

List any other skills you have:

_____

_____

_____

_____

Interaction

Ask another student these questions about his or her job. Fill in the information on the chart below.

Where are you working now?	
Exactly what do you do?	
How long have you been there?	
What other jobs have you had? What were your responsibilities?	
How long were you there?	
Tell me about your education or any special training you've had.	
What other skills do you have?	

Discuss

The following is a list of reasons a person may have for leaving or changing a job. Sit in a small group and talk about each reason. Check the ones you think are acceptable to give at an interview. Add one more acceptable reason.

_____ I don't like the job I have.

_____ I'm looking for a position where there is room for advancement.

_____ I was laid off because business is slow.

_____ I didn't get along with my boss.

_____ I'm bored with my job.

_____ I want to work on a job that is more interesting.

_____ My job is 60 miles from my house. I'd like to find something closer to home.

_____ My job is 60 miles from my house. I have trouble getting to work on time.

_____ The pay is low.

_____ I was fired.

_____ We moved here because my husband/wife got a job in this area.

_____ I hurt my back and I'm unable to do heavy work.

_____ _____

Role play

It is important to explain your personal strengths at a job interview. Employers are looking for people with the qualities listed below. Write a personal example for each of the following statements. Then sit in a small group and share your sentences with the other students.

1. I work well with other people. _____

_____

2. I'm hard working. _____

_____

3. I take on extra responsibility. _____

_____

4. I communicate well. _____

_____

5. I'm organized. _____

_____

6. _____

_____

Linn is at a job interview for an assistant store manager. Sit in a small group and discuss each statement. Write "should" or "shouldn't" in the blank.

1. How should she dress and act at the interview?

   a. She _____ arrive a half hour early for the interview.

   b. She _____ wear jeans.

   c. She _____ make eye contact with the interviewer.

   d. She _____ shake hands with the interviewer when she arrives and leaves.

2. How should she answer, "Tell me about your job now?"

   a. She _____ explain the daily responsibilities of her job in detail.

   b. She _____ talk about the problems that she's having with her supervisor.

   c. She _____ explain that she sometimes takes on extra responsibilities and give examples.

3. How should she answer, "Have you had any other experience?"

   a. She _____ talk about the job she had in her country.

   b. She _____ talk about the housekeeping job that she had when she first came to this country.

   c. She _____ tell about her role as treasurer of the Parent's Organization at her child's school.

4. How should she answer, "Why do you want to change jobs?"

   a. She _____ explain that she wants a higher salary.

   b. She _____ explain that there are very few opportunities for advancement at her present job.

   c. She _____ explain that she wants more responsibility and challenge.

5. How should she answer, "Do you have any questions to ask us?"

   a. Her first question _____ be, "What are the salary and benefits?"

   b. She _____ ask about the responsibilities of the new job.

   c. Before she accepts the job, she _____ be sure that she understands the salary and benefits.

6. How should she answer, "Do you have anything else you would like to tell us about yourself?"

   a. She _____ talk about her childcare problems.

   b. She _____ tell the interviewer that she's going to school at night and studying English and business.

   c. She _____ say that she's hardworking and very organized.

With another student, write and practice a job interview between an employer and a person applying for a job. Use these questions to help you with the conversation. Present your dialogue to the class.

Employer questions:

1. What types of training and experience do you have that relate to this job?
2. What are your major strengths?
3. What are your major weaknesses?
4. What did you like most and least about your last job?
5. Why do you want to leave your job?
6. Have you ever had difficulty getting along with coworkers?
7. What do you know about this company?
8. What are your plans for the future?
9. What are your hobbies and interests? How do you spend your free time?
10. What else would you like to tell me about yourself?

Applicant questions:

1. What are the responsibilities of the job?
2. What would a typical day be like?
3. What is the greatest challenge of this job?
4. Are there opportunities for job training or continuing my education?
5. Are there opportunities for advancement in the company?

AUTOBODY—busy shop needs painter's helper & light bodywork. Exp a must. Call 659-8112.

AUTO MECHANIC

Immed opening for qualified indiv. Must be exp'd in brakes, suspension, alignment, exhaust, tune-up diagnosis and repair. ASE certified pref'd. Call 233-0988.

BUS OPERATORS –

Excel oppty for FT/PT work, 1 yr. exp w/ transit or coach buses. Must have clean DL record. 431-6464 ask for Tom.

CARPET INSTALLER -

Exp'd helpers and mechanics. FT/PT. Tools and own trans req'd.
Call 299-9374

COMPUTER OPERATOR

FT for local accounting office. Fax résumé to 638-874-8873.

DRIVER

For step van, for delivery to supermarkets. Good benefits. Professional attitude and good driving record req. Call 443-8787 for appt.

ELECTRICIAN/ MECHANIC HELPERS

Exp in residential wiring. Top pay, steady work, OT. Health ins and benefits Call 877-1214.

ENGINEER / CIVIL

Established engineering firm seeking graduate Civil Engineer with design exp in roadway, bridges, and sewers. F/T position w/ exc benefits.
Call 549-9437.

HOME HEALTH AIDES
CERTIFIED

Well established home health care agency has immediate positions for certified home health aides on private cases at home. Choice of hours, weekdays/weekends. Minimum 1 year exp req.
Call 673-3442.

MECHANICS

Class A or B Mechanics needed for fleet maintenance/repairs. Valid driver's license, good driving record reqd. FT w/ benefits. Mon–Fri 5 AM-2PM. Call Sharon at 544-3388.

NURSES, RN and LPN

Area nursing home, quality long term care, seeking nurses for second and third shift. Exc. benefits. 344-6221

PROGRAMMER/ANALYST

Immediate opening. Must have BS in computer science. Job involves network installs, programming, technical customer support. Fax résumé to 439-844-2713.

RETAIL SALES High quality audio store needs motivated individual to sell quality home and car stereo equipment. Exp pref or will train right person. Excel pay and benefits.
Call 411-8733.

SALES Furniture Wholesaler is seeking an enthusiastic, hard-working representative to cover sales throughout state. Exp in outside sales necessary. Spanish-speaking a plus. Call 225-7744.

SECURITY OFFICERS
IMMEDIATE OPENINGS

Fantastic opportunity for individuals who take pride in their work. Above average wages and benefits. Car, home phone, high school diplomas or GED a must. Clean police record. Apply in person. 1233 Morris Ave, Bayville.

TEACHER OF THE HANDICAPPED

Immediate opening in private school. Must have certification. Fax résumé to 377-765-2000.

TRAVEL AGENT

New office opening in Coopertown. Min 2 years exp. System 1a+. Call Patty at 533-0808.

Discuss these questions using the classified ads above.

1. Which jobs require a license or certificate?
2. Which companies will train new employees?
3. Which jobs do not require experience?
4. Which jobs require special skills?
5. Which jobs offer benefits?
7. Which jobs require a college degree?
8. Which ads require a résumé?
9. Which jobs request that the applicant fax a résumé?
10. Choose a job which you are interested in and which you are qualified for. Explain why.

complete

Complete the information on the résumé worksheet about yourself. Describe your education and work experience.

RÉSUMÉ WORKSHEET

_____ (name)

_____ (address)

_____

_____ (phone number)

OBJECTIVE: Write the kind of position you are looking for.

_____

EDUCATION: List the schools you have attended. Include dates and subject areas you studied, starting with your most recent school.

___ to ___   _____

_____

___ to ___   _____

_____

EXPERIENCE: List the names of jobs, places, dates, and descriptions of exactly what you did, starting with your most recent job.

___ to ___   _____

_____

___ to ___   _____

_____

___ to ___   _____

_____

SPECIAL SKILLS: List any other information which you think might be helpful. Examples: special skills, hobbies, organizations, community services, languages you speak.

_____

_____

REFERENCES: List names and addresses of two or three references or write "References available on request."

_____

13 A Robbery

Discuss

Was your home ever broken into or robbed? What happened?
Did you report the robbery to the police? What did they do?
How can you prevent a robbery in your home?

Read

Somewhere in the United States, there is a robbery every ten seconds. Do you know what to do if your house or car is broken into? Do you know how to make it harder for thieves to steal your car or rob your house?

First, if you arrive home and suspect that a robber is inside, do not enter. It could be dangerous for you to go into the house and surprise the robber. Call the police from a safe place. When the police come, they will go into your home and check to see if it is safe.

If you discover that your car or home has been broken into or robbed, you should report it to the police immediately. In most cases, a police officer will come to the scene of the crime and investigate. It is important not to touch or clean anything before the police come. They will want to examine the area for any clues which might help them. They will also want to know exactly what was stolen. As soon as possible after the robbery, make a list of everything that was taken. If you have insurance, report the robbery to them, too. The insurance company might also send someone to investigate.

Robberies and break-ins can often be prevented. Good locks on all windows and doors will keep out many thieves. If you plan to be away, be sure to stop mail, newspapers, and other deliveries. An automatic timer to turn lights on and off during the day and evening will make your home appear occupied. By taking precautions, you can significantly reduce the chances of being robbed.

Read each sentence. If it is true, write T. If it is false, write F.

_____ 1. If your front door is open when you get home, go inside and call the police.

_____ 2. You should report a break-in to the police even if nothing was taken.

_____ 3. Cleaning up before the police arrive could destroy evidence such as fingerprints.

_____ 4. Locking your doors will prevent all robberies.

_____ 5. Before you go away on vacation, it's a good idea to set a timer to turn on some lights at 6 P. M. and shut them off at 11:30 P. M..

Clara: I don't believe this mess! I was only away overnight.
Police: What was taken?
Clara: My stereo. And my gold ring and necklace were stolen, too.
Police: Was anything damaged?
Clara: My sofa was torn and my bedroom was ransacked. How do you think they got into my apartment?
Police: It looks like they got in through the window. Did you lock your windows before you left?
Clara: I'm not sure. I think so.
Police: You should always check your windows before you leave. And you should've asked your neighbor to pick up your newspaper. It was still lying in front of the door when I came in.

Practice this model with the pictures below.

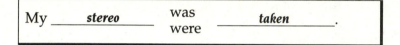

| My _____*stereo*_____ | was
were | _____*taken*_____ . |

1. stereo / take

2. diamond ring / steal

3. lamps / break

4. TV and camera / take

5. necklace and gold ring / steal

6. living room furniture / damage

7. bedroom / ransack

9. credit cards / steal

8. CD player and VCR / take

Partner Exercise

Talk about each robbery.

Student 1

stereo / take
My stereo was taken.

1. stereo / take
2. TV and camera / take
3. jewelry / steal
4. computer / damage
5. gold necklace and diamond ring / steal
6. lamps / break
7. $250 in cash / take
8. living room / ransack
9. CD player and CDs / steal
10. bedroom furniture / damage

(FOLD HERE)

Student 2
Listen carefully and help Student 1.

1. My stereo was taken.
2. My TV and camera were taken.
3. My jewelry was stolen.
4. My computer was damaged.
5. My gold necklace and diamond ring were stolen.
6. My lamps were broken.
7. $250 in cash was taken.
8. My living room was ransacked.
9. My CD player and CDs were stolen.
10. My bedroom furniture was damaged.

Complete these conversations between a police officer and the victim of a robbery.

Victim: My apartment _____ into (break) while I was away for the weekend.

Police: What _____ (steal)?

Victim: My brand new TV and VCR _____ (take).

Police: _____ anything else _____ (take)?

Victim: Luckily, only my costume jewelry _____ (steal). They couldn't find my good jewelry or my cash.

Victim: I can't believe my house _____ (rob). I was away on vacation and just got back this afternoon.

Police: What _____ (take)?

Victim: My best jewelry _____ (take), my pearl necklace, three rings, and a gold bracelet. And $300 in cash _____ (steal).

Police: _____ anything else _____ (take)?

Victim: No, but my bedroom and living room _____ (ransack). My furniture _____ (damage) and the lamps _____ (break). It's a mess!

84

Tom's house was broken into while he was on vacation. Practice this model and talk about what he should have done to prevent the robbery.

He should've _____ *locked all the windows* _____ before he went away.

1. lock all the windows

2. ask a neighbor to check his house

3. keep on a radio with a timer

4. ask a friend to pick up his mail

5. stop all deliveries

6. leave on a light with a timer

Partner Exercise

Talk about what these people should have done before they went away on vacation.

Student 1	**Student 2**
You / lock your doors	*Listen carefully and help Student 1.*
You should have locked your doors.	

Student 1

1. You / lock your doors
2. He / stop the mail
3. She / install an alarm system

4. You / speak to a friend
5. He / cancel the newspaper

6. They / leave on a light with a timer
7. We / ask someone to cut our lawn

(FOLD HERE)

Student 2

1. You should've locked your doors.
2. He should've stopped the mail .
3. She should've installed an alarm system.
4. You should've spoken to a friend.
5. He should've canceled the newspaper.
6. They should've left on a light with a timer.
7. We should've asked someone to cut our lawn.

Sit in a small group. The following sentences give suggestions about making your house safe when you are away. After you read each one and discuss it, write "should" or "shouldn't" in the blank.

1. You _____ put on a light with a timer when you go away.

2. You _____ leave the TV on while you are away.

3. You _____ install double locks on your doors before you leave on vacation.

4. You _____ tell all your neighbors before you go to Europe on business.

5. You _____ leave an extra apartment key under the doormat when you go away for the weekend.

6. You _____ keep all the lights on when you go away overnight.

7. You _____ ask a neighbor to water your outside plants when you go away for two weeks.

8. You _____ stop your mail before you go on vacation.

9. You _____ ask a friend to pick up any newspapers or advertisements delivered to your door.

10. You _____ leave a window open for ventilation when you go away in the summer.

Interaction

Sit in a small group. Ask one student these questions about a robbery. Fill in the answers on the chart below.

1. Who was robbed?	
2. When was the robbery?	
3. What was taken?	
4. Was anything damaged?	
5. How did the robber get in?	
6. Were the police called?	
7. What finally happened?	

Koji and Kyoko went back to Japan for two weeks to visit their families. While they were away, their home was robbed. Sit in a group and talk about the picture. What should or shouldn't they have done before they went on vacation? Write seven suggestions under the picture.

1. _____

2. _____

3. _____

4. _____

5. _____

6. _____

7. _____

Role play

Write and practice a conversation between a police officer and a person whose house was robbed. Describe the robbery in detail. Talk about what this person should have done to prevent it. Present your conversation to the class.

14 United States Government

Discuss

What is a democracy? What rights do people have in a democracy? What are the differences between the U.S. system of government and the government in your country?

Read

After the American Revolution, the United States became an independent country. A few years later, in 1787, the U.S. Constitution was written and approved by the states. The Constitution established a democratic system of government which divided power among the three branches of the government, the legislative, executive, and judicial branches, to make sure that no single branch could become too powerful. The Constitution also gave specific rights and freedoms to all people who live in the United States.

The legislative branch, usually called Congress, has two parts, the House of Representatives and the Senate. They are responsible for writing all laws. In the House of Representatives, states with more people have more representatives than states with less people. In the Senate, however, each of the fifty states, large or small, has two senators.

The executive branch is led by the president and vice president who can be elected for a maximum of two four-year terms. This branch includes all the departments and agencies of the U.S. government and is responsible for carrying out all laws. The president suggests bills to Congress. After a bill passes the House and Senate, the president has a choice of signing the bill into law or vetoing the bill and sending it back to Congress.

The third part of the U.S. government is the judicial branch. The judicial branch consists of the Supreme Court and lower federal courts. The nine members of the Supreme Court are appointed by the president for life. The Supreme Court decides if lower court decisions, state laws, and federal laws are consistent with the Constitution.

Read each sentence. If it is true, write T. If it is false, write F.

_____ 1. The U.S. Constitution created three branches of government.

_____ 2. There are two representatives from each state in the House of Representatives.

_____ 3. The members of the Supreme Court are elected every four years.

_____ 4. The president has to sign a bill passed by Congress.

_____ 5. The Supreme Court can decide that a law passed by Congress and signed by the president is unconstitutional.

THE BILL OF RIGHTS

The Bill of Rights is the first ten Amendments of the U.S. Constitution. Read each amendment with your teacher and discuss how the amendment affects people's lives in the United States.

Discuss

AMENDMENT I: Freedom of religion, speech, press, assembly, and petition.

AMENDMENT II: Right to keep and have guns. The need for a military.

AMENDMENT III: No placing of soldiers in private homes.

AMENDMENT IV: No unreasonable searches and seizures.

AMENDMENT V: Right not to go to trial twice for the same crime and not to answer questions at your own trial. Protection of private property.

AMENDMENT VI: Right to a speedy trial by jury and to question witnesses. Right to a lawyer.

AMENDMENT VII: Right to a jury trial for civil cases.

AMENDMENT VIII: No excessive bail, or cruel and unusual punishment

AMENDMENT IX: People's rights are not limited to those listed in the Constitution.

AMENDMENT X: Powers not given to the federal government belong to the states or the people.

Write the number of the amendment that gives you the following rights or freedoms.

_____ 1. People can practice any religion they want to.

_____ 2. A soldier cannot ask to stay in your home.

_____ 3. People can sign a petition to change a law and give the petition to the government officials.

_____ 4. Police cannot come into your house without a search warrant.

_____ 5. A newspaper can print articles disagreeing with government policies.

_____ 6. Depending on the crime, an arrested person can usually pay a reasonable amount of bail to leave jail until his or her trial.

_____ 7. People can demonstrate in the street.

_____ 8. People can keep licensed guns in their houses.

_____ 9. A person can get a public defender if he or she does not have enough money for a lawyer.

_____10. If a person goes to trial and is found not guilty, the person cannot go to trial again for the same crime.

_____11. Each state can pass laws about marriage, divorce, education, and state taxes because these areas are not covered by federal laws.

_____12. A defendant (a person arrested) will have a trial by jury if the defendant pleads not guilty.

THE THREE BRANCHES OF GOVERNMENT

LEGISLATIVE BRANCH - THE CONGRESS

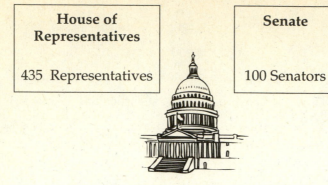

House of Representatives

435 Representatives

Senate

100 Senators

- writes and passes laws
- confirms judges, Cabinet members, directors of federal agencies
- declares war

EXECUTIVE BRANCH - THE PRESIDENT

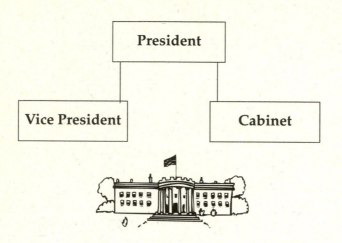

President

Vice President

Cabinet

- suggests laws
- signs or vetoes laws
- appoints judges, heads of federal agencies, and ambassadors
- commands the military
- conducts relations with foreign countries

JUDICIAL BRANCH - THE COURTS

**The Supreme Court
1 Chief Justice**

8 Associate Justices

Federal Courts

- hears appeals to determine if laws are constitutional
- reviews decisions made by lower courts
- hears federal civil rights cases
- hears cases involving crimes against the government

Read the responsibilities of the three branches of government. Practice this model and talk about the duties of each branch.

A: Which branch of the government _____*suggests laws*_____ ?

B: The _____*executive branch*_____ does .

LEGISLATIVE BRANCH–THE HOUSE OF REPRESENTATIVES

The House of Representatives has 435 members. The number of representatives for each state is based on each state's population. The states with the largest populations have the most representatives and the ones with the lowest populations have the least number. Every ten years, the number of representatives for each state changes depending on the census statistics. The next censuses will be in the years 2000, 2010, and 2020. The map below lists each state's population in 1994 and the number of representatives for each state.

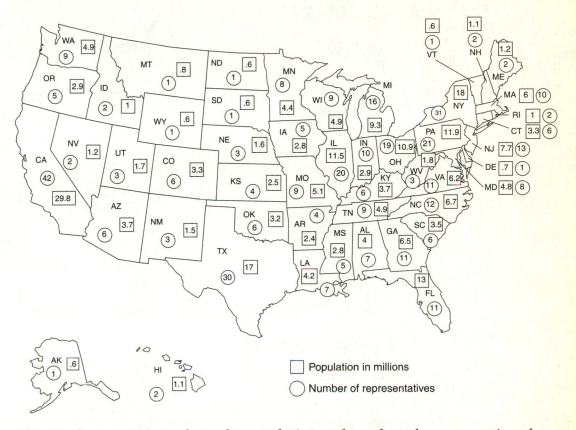

Discuss these questions about the population and number of representatives from each state.

1. Which states have more than 20 representatives?
2. Which states have less than four representatives?
3. Alaska is the largest state geographically. Does it have the most representatives?
4. Which state has the most representatives?
5. What's the population of the state with the most representatives?
6. Rhode Island is the smallest state geographically. Does it have the lowest number of representatives?
7. Which states have only one representative? What is the population of these states?
8. What is the population of your state? How many representatives do you have?

EXECUTIVE BRANCH

The following are the results of the 1992 presidential election. Discuss the results with your teacher.

Candidates	Party	Number of Votes (Popular Vote)	% of vote	Number of States Won	Electoral Votes
Clinton / Gore	Democratic	44.9 million	43%	30	370
Bush / Quayle	Republican	39.1 million	38%	20	105
Perot/Stockdale	Independent	19.7 million	19%	0	0

The following are the results of the 1992 presidential election. Discuss the results with your teacher.

__Clinton and Gore__ received __44.9 million__ popular votes.
_____ received _____ percent of the vote.
_____ won _____ states.
_____ received _____ electoral votes.

Complete this information about the last presidential election.

1. The last presidential election was in _____.

2. The candidates and their parties were:

   Candidates: _____ Party: _____

   Candidates: _____ Party: _____

   Candidates: _____ Party: _____

3. _____ won the election.

4. Was the election close or was it a landslide victory?

   _____

5. Three important issues in the campaign were:

   _____

   _____

   _____

Go Find Out *Find out the following information about your current federal, state, and local government.*

FEDERAL GOVERNMENT

1. Who are the senators from your state and what parties are they in?

   Senator: _____ Party: _____

   Senator: _____ Party: _____

2. How many congressmen or congresswomen does your state have? _____

3. Who is your congressman or congresswoman in the House of Representatives? _____

   Representative: _____ Party: _____

STATE GOVERNMENT

1. What state do you live in? _____

2. What is your state capital? _____

3. What's the population of your state? _____

4. Who is the governor of your state?
   Governor: _____ Party: _____

5. Who are your local representatives to your state legislature?

   Representative: _____ Party: _____

   Representative: _____ Party: _____

LOCAL GOVERNMENT

1. What county do you live in? _____

2. What city do you live in? _____

3. Who is the mayor of your town or city?

   Mayor: _____ Party: _____

4. Who is your representative to your town or city council?

   Representative: _____ Party: _____

15 The Telephone

Discuss

How do you feel when you speak in
English on the telephone?
Do you have an answering machine?
What do you do when you call a
business and get an answering
machine?

Read

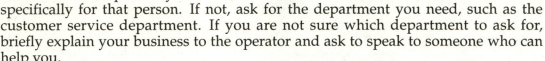

When you make a call to a business
or agency, it is sometimes difficult to get
the person or department you want. In
some companies, telephone calls are
answered by a company operator who
directs the calls to the proper
department or extension. If you know
the name of the person you want, ask
specifically for that person. If not, ask for the department you need, such as the
customer service department. If you are not sure which department to ask for,
briefly explain your business to the operator and ask to speak to someone who can
help you.

In many companies, you will reach an automated answering service. It
requires careful listening to follow the taped message. The caller is asked to press
#1 for one department, press #2 for a different department, and so on. If you can
follow the message and hear the department you need, press the appropriate
number. If you don't hear the department you need, the last part of the tape will
often say, "Stay on the line for operator assistance" or "Press #____ if you need
assistance."

Finally, many small businesses and individuals have answering machines.
After a short introduction, the tape asks the caller to listen for the beep, then to
leave a short message. Leave your name, telephone number, and reason for calling.
Be sure to include the time that you can be reached.

Read each statement. If it is true, write T. If it is false, write F.

_____ 1. A person always answers the phone when you call a business.

_____ 2. If you don't understand an automated message, hang up immediately.

_____ 3. When a telephone operator answers, explain who or what you want.

_____ 4. Sometimes you need to press a number on the phone to get the
information that you need.

_____ 5. When you leave a message, say your name slowly and clearly.

Machine:	Thank you for calling Bell Tel.
	If you have a question about your bill, press 1.
	If you are calling about a new installation, press 2.
	If you are calling about a change or addition in service, press 3.
Mira:	(Presses #2)
Operator:	Bell Tel. Paula speaking. How can I help you?
Mira:	I'm moving to this city next week and I'll need a phone.
	Can you tell me how much your monthly service charge is?
Operator:	$21.50 and that includes unlimited local calling.
Mira:	How much is the installation?
Operator:	That's $26.
Mira:	That sounds fine. Now, what information do you need?

Practice Practice

Practice both question models and ask for the information below.

How much is the monthly service charge	?

Can you tell me		
I'd like to know	*how much the monthly service charge is*	?

1. How much / monthly service charge

2. How much / ticket

3. When / visiting hours

4. When / interview

5. When / next bus

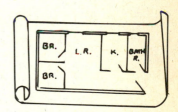

6. Where / apartment

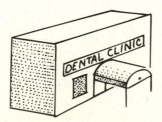

4. Where / doctor's office

5. What / his phone number

6. What / their address

Practice both question models and ask for the information below.

| When does the store open | ? |

| Can you tell me | | |
| I'd like to know | when the store opens | ? |

1. When / open

2. When / close

3. When / expire

4. Where / live

5. Where / work

6. How often / shuttle to Boston / leave

Ask questions on the telephone.

Partner Exercise

Student 1	**Student 2**
What time / the store / open?	*Listen carefully and help Student 1.*
What time does the store open?	

1. What time / the store /open?
2. Can you tell me / what time / the store / open?
3. How much /the course /cost?
4. Can you tell me / how much / the course / cost?
5. When / my policy /expire?
6. Can you tell me / when / my policy / expire?
7. How many rooms / the apartment / have?
8. Can you tell me / how many rooms / the apartment / have?
9. What / be / my balance?
10. Can you tell me / what / my balance / be?

(FOLD HERE)

1. What time does the store open?
2. Can you tell me what time the store opens?
3. How much does the course cost?
4. Can you tell me how much the course costs?
5. When does my policy expire?
6. Can you tell me when my policy expires?
7. How many rooms does the apartment have?
8. Can you tell me how many rooms the apartment has?
9. What is my balance?
10. Can you tell me what my balance is?

96

Complete these telephone conversations.

Clerk:	Rollins Rentals.
Charles:	I'd like some information about renting a car.
Clerk:	Of course.
Charles:	Can you tell me _____ ?
Clerk:	It's $58 a day.
Charles:	Are there any additional charges?
Clerk:	_____ .
Charles:	What time _____ ?
Clerk:	We open at 7:00 a.m.

Clerk:	Health Department.
Ms. Van:	I'd like some information about getting immunizations for my son.
Clerk:	Yes.
Ms. Van:	Can you tell me _____ ?
Clerk:	Yes, we give measles, mumps and polio.
Ms. Van:	When _____ ?
Clerk:	On the first and third Monday of the month, at 9:00 A.M.

 **Find Out**

The following are questions you can ask on the telephone to find out information about companies and services in your area. In a small group, decide on two additional places in your area and write a question for each. Then call one of the places below and ask for the information requested. Remember to thank the person you speak to. Talk about your calls with the class.

Place	Question
Library	Can you tell me what your hours are?
Bank	Could you tell me what the interest rate on a one-year CD is?
Post Office	I'd like to know what your hours are.
Hospital	Could you tell me what the visiting hours are?
Telephone Company	Can you tell me how much it costs to add call waiting to my service?
Cable	I'd like to know how much basic cable service is.
Train	Can you tell me when I can get a train to _____?

Thank you for calling Suburban Cable.

For account balances, press 1.

For repair service, press 2.

To order a movie, press 3.

To begin service with Suburban Cable, press 4.

For customer service, press 5.

You are calling the cable TV service in your area. Match each situation with one of the choices above. Write the number you would press.

_____ 1. You would like cable TV installed in your home.

_____ 2. You're not sure how much your bill is this month.

_____ 3. You want to find the cheapest package the cable company offers.

_____ 4. You would like to see a pay-per-view movie tomorrow night.

_____ 5. The picture on your screen isn't clear.

_____ 6. You want to find out how much it will cost to add a sports channel to your service.

In a small group, discuss these questions.

1. What companies in your area have an automated answering service?
2. When was the last time you heard an automated service? What company were you calling?
3. Did you hang up? Did you stay on the line and press one of the choices? Did you get the information you wanted?
4. What should you do if you don't understand the choices?
5. How do you feel when you hear an automated service?

> A & S Electric. I can't come to the phone right now. Please leave your name and phone number and a brief message. I'll get back to you as soon as possible. Thank you for calling.

> This is Emily Lang. I need two new outlets in the living room. Please call me at 483-9291. You can reach me after 5:00. Thanks.

Work in a small group. You are calling the small companies below. Leave a brief message.

1. Thank you for calling King's Plumbing. We aren't in the office right now. After the beep, please leave your name, phone number, and a brief message. I'll return your call shortly.

_____

_____

_____

2. This is Marin Management. No one is in the office now. If you leave your name and number and message, we'll get back to you as soon as possible.

_____

_____

_____

3. You have reached Southside Movers. At the tone, please leave a message, including your name and number. We'll return your call today.

_____

_____

_____

4. You have just bought an answering machine. Write the message you will record on your machine.

_____

_____

_____

Appendix

Common Irregular Verbs

Base Form	Past	Past Participle
be	was, were	been
begin	began	begun
break	broke	broken
bring	brought	brought
buy	bought	bought
come	came	come
cut	cut	cut
do	did	done
drink	drank	drunk
drive	drove	driven
eat	ate	eaten
fall	fell	fallen
feel	felt	felt
find	found	found
forget	forgot	forgotten
get	got	got *or* gotten
give	gave	given
go	went	gone
have	had	had
hear	heard	heard
hurt	hurt	hurt
know	knew	know
leave	left	left
lend	lent	lent
lose	lost	lost
make	made	made
pay	paid	paid
put	put	put
run	ran	run
say	said	said
see	saw	seen
sell	sold	sold
send	sent	sent
speak	spoke	spoke
spend	spent	spent
stand	stood	stood
steal	stole	stolen
take	took	taken
tell	told	told
throw	throw	thrown
win	won	won
write	wrote	written